Bishop of the Barrio

Bishop of the Barrio

The Life of Bishop Alphonse Gallegos, OAR

John Oldfield, OAR

With a Foreword by Bishop Francis A. Quinn
and an Afterword from Cardinal Roger Mahony

PAULIST PRESS
New York/Mahwah, N.J.

Interior photos courtesy of the Augustinian Recollects archives, West Orange, NJ; family photo p. 41 courtesy of Senaida Kane.
Homily by Cardinal Roger Mahony pp. 81–85 reprinted from *The Catholic Herald,* October 16, 1991, p. 10.

Cover design by Sharyn Banks
Book design by Lynn Else

Library of Congress Cataloging-in-Publication Data

    Oldfield, John, OAR.
    Bishop of the barrio : the life of Bishop Alphonse Gallegos, OAR / John Oldfield ; with a foreword by Francis A. Quinn ; and an afterword from Roger Mahony.
       p. cm.
    Includes bibliographical references (p.   ).
    ISBN 0-8091-4430-1 (alk. paper)
    1. Gallegos, Alphonse, 1931-1991. 2. Catholic Church—California—Bishops—Biography. I. Title.
    BX4705.G1495O53 2007
    282.092—dc22
    [B]

                              2006015209

Published by Paulist Press
997 Macarthur Boulevard
Mahwah, New Jersey 07430

www.paulistpress.com

Printed and bound in the
United States of America

Contents

Foreword

I first came to know Bishop Alphonse Gallegos when he was director of Hispanic affairs for the California Catholic Conference in Sacramento. I later learned of Father Al's boyhood in Albuquerque, his studies for the Augustinian priesthood, and eventually his exceptional and effective ministry in Los Angeles. The personal magnetism, the courage and persistence in overcoming obstacles that he evidenced in those earlier years came to full development in his role as auxiliary bishop of the Diocese of Sacramento in 1981.

Particularly because of his warm, outgoing personality, Bishop Al was immediately accepted by this Northern California diocesan community. Young people found a friend in the new bishop, who showed a genuine interest in them in St. Rose Parish, where he resided, and in the adjacent St. Patrick's School. In short time, he had become identified with the lowriders, mixing with them and their customized cars on the streets of Sacramento. The bonding of a church representative with Latino and other youths, so urgently needed, would endure to the end of the bishop's life.

If one were to categorize this man, the term that would spring to mind would be "people-priest." As pastor of Our Lady of Guadalupe Parish and as auxiliary bishop, he continually looked for means to encourage young and old, to assist individuals financially, to counsel troubled marriages—to do what Jesus did: teach, preach, heal, and reconcile.

Personally, I was blessed to have a colleague bishop collaborative and supportive in every way. I learned from him in his prayerfulness, his faithfulness to priestly obligations and devotions, his love for the Blessed Mother. Most of all, I was impressed by Bishop Al's courage. This was a man who struggled against a serious visual impairment since childhood, finally to excel in the demanding vocations of priest and bishop—always joyful, and never with self-pity or complaint.

My life benefited enormously from Alphonse Gallegos's example—as I know did the life of every person whom he encountered. The outpouring of affection at his funeral was an unparalleled tribute to a bishop who had died doing what he always did, helping others.

Francis A. Quinn
Bishop of the Diocese of Sacramento (retired)

CHAPTER 1

![decorative band of triangular shapes]

Early Years

Doctors' Hospital Case No. FF 846

A formal, archival document described as "Doctors' Hospital Case No. FF 846"[1] refers to a Mr. A.G., a youthful patient, as a case of "extreme myopia." The contact of A.G. with the specialists at Doctors' Hospital, Los Angeles, California, took place when the patient was sixteen years of age. His parents had hoped that, by means of the constant corrections of the lenses of his glasses, which had been worn since a very early age, their son's weak vision might be improved. Such was not the case. An otherwise healthy youth was condemned to near sightlessness, an inhibiting myopic condition that required that he attend sight-saving classes in school and that he avoid the normal rough-and-tumble sports enjoyed by other youths his age.

The doctors recommended radical surgery. Over a period of two years, A.G. underwent two very delicate surgical procedures on his eyes, performed in accordance with the new techniques developed by the renowned Spanish ophthalmologist, Dr. Ramón Castroviejo. The results were promising. Before surgery, the report states, "Without glasses, his vision was such that he could read print at two inches from either eye....At ten inches, he was unable to count fingers." Following the surgeries, his vision, still dependent upon corrective lenses, had improved to such an extent that, as the report reads, "He is now out of sight saving classes and is attending regular city schools."

The A.G. of whom Dr. H. G. Blasdel speaks in Hospital Case No. FF 846 was Alphonse Gallegos, future Roman Catholic auxiliary bishop of the Diocese of Sacramento, and outstanding religious leader in the development of the apostolate among the Spanish-speaking and other minority groups in the state of California. The satisfaction of the Los Angeles doctor of ophthalmology was shared by the future bishop and his family. It had been a professional accomplishment and meant a return to a degree of normalcy in the life of a young man who had a deep-seated desire to fulfill, a desire to become a priest and a religious.

The Gallegos Family from Albuquerque to Watts

Normalcy for the young Alphonse was, at that time, life with his parents, Joseph (José) Gallegos and Caciana Apodaca, and with a house full of brothers and sisters—eleven siblings in all: Sally, Leonard, Ralph, Senaida, Arlene, Evangeline, Rita, Alphonse and his twin, Eloy, Raymond, and Lina. Alphonse was born in Albuquerque, New Mexico, on February 20, 1931, and was baptized four days later in Sacred Heart Church as "Alfonso Napoleon." He would be confirmed as an infant in the same church on December 6, also in 1931. The Gallegos and Apodaca families had deep roots in New Mexico, a state in which the culture of old Spain and Mexico had been maintained even following its annexation to the westward-expanding United States in 1848.[2] Although the parents had many ties to their state and particularly to Albuquerque, they decided to venture to new surroundings and opportunities in California shortly after the birth of Alphonse.

The 1930s had been a time of migrations to the Golden State and the satellite communities of greater Los Angeles from all over the United States. Farmers, workers, and their families sought better opportunities in their efforts to survive the effects of the Great Depression. Perhaps the move of the Gallegos family to Watts was one of those secret promptings of the Holy Spirit that lay beyond the surface in the history of humanity's migrations. The mother of the young Gallegos family, Caciana, was particularly motivated by a desire for better educational opportunities for her children. One opportunity that also presented itself to the family was the contact with Doctors' Hospital. Alphonse's parents, solicitous of their son's delicate eyesight, had promptly sent him to sight-saving classes; already from the age of nine he was wearing eyeglasses with very thick lenses. One can imagine the kind of stigma this might have been, considering that streak of thoughtless cruelty that children sometimes display in different forms of ridicule. If Alphonse had received such treatment, it would never be known. He had a hallmark smile that could overcome any such mockery or rejection. And, certainly, he would never have experienced such treatment at home. His father, Joseph, a carpenter, and his mother, Caciana, in addition to searching for the right medical care for their son, created a home atmosphere of love and religious piety that gave the children love's security and unity.

The rhythm of life in the Gallegos household included the afternoon homework and catechetical instructions, with the older children responsible for teaching the younger the basics of prayer and Christian doctrine. Following the evening meal, all gathered to recite the rosary, a daily event. Joseph, the carpenter-father, had made benches like those of a small chapel for use at prayer time. It was a very united family in which the parents set the example of cheerful piety. Early on, around 1934, they had chosen Saint Joseph as their patron and as their father's special protector. The family believes, even today, that, due to this devotion, their father, a skilled carpenter, never lacked for work. The annual celebration of the feast of Saint Joseph at 11007 Watts Avenue was a neighborhood event to which all were invited.

The hope that constantly motivated their efforts to care for the eleven children and to seek all the help that they could for Alphonse's extremely limited eyesight rested in their devotion to Saint Joseph, another carpenter and patron saint of the family. And, of course, special assistance was sought from Saint Lucy, the patroness of the blind. The network of prayer and spiritual encouragement included the faithful of the little parish church of San Miguel, home to the Mexican and Mexican American population of Watts. The parish became the spiritual center of what came to be a *barrio,* the Spanish word for "neighborhood." It was the custom of the Hispanic immigrants to refer to those neighborhoods where Spanish was spoken and where shops, restaurants, and other local institutions reflected their cultural tastes as barrios.

A Word about Watts

In the early 1800s, the area now known as Watts had been called "Rancho Tajuate," a region of ranches and fruit orchards. It received the name of "Watts" from Mrs. Julius Watts, owner of a large ranch in the area, who provided the land for the construction of an important railroad station and yards. The coming of the railroad changed the rural character of the area, making way for a neighborhood of small houses on the edge of an expanding Los Angeles. The family recalls the area as a mixed community with various neighbors of Greek, Russian, and German background.

Watts in the 1930s became home to a growing community of Mexican and Mexican American migrants. Some of the former migrant group were those Mexicans known as *Cristeros* who had fled from the religious persecutions that had afflicted the church in Mexico in the '20s and early '30s. As an important railroad center, Watts offered job opportunities to the newcomers. In a similar manner, many African Americans would come to Watts and the surrounding areas during World War II in search of employment in the defense industries so important in that era. Watts would become nationally known in the 1960s as the scene of riots and civil rights agitation. In the midst of these changing demographics, the Latino barrio retained its ethnic identity and sought sources of solidarity such as a neighborhood Catholic Church, which would be San Miguel, named after the more affluent sponsoring parish, St. Michael the Archangel in south central Los Angeles. The new church dedicated to the archangel came into existence in December 1927. The first pastor was a priest from Mexico, Father Salvador Martinez Silva, who guided the faithful in their efforts to create community and to ensure the transmission of their religious and cultural heritage to the next generation. The Gallegos family would be among the pioneer families of this new parish in the heart of Watts.

CHAPTER 2

Seeing with the Heart

The Cultivation of a Vocation

Young Alphonse came into contact with the Augustinian Recollects, a Roman Catholic religious order of Spanish origin that had come to Watts and San Miguel in 1929. The Spanish priests of the order were on the threshold of a renewed apostolate to the Spanish-speaking in the land of Blessed Junipero Serra's famous missions. It had been quite a historical leap from the *camino real* of the missions to Hollywood, but the Recollect newcomers to Watts could take secret pleasure in the abundance of Spanish place names for avenues, boulevards, and towns as well as wince at the anglicized pronunciations of the same.

Spanish was spoken in Watts, but Alphonse did not speak very much Spanish as a child. After all, his family was more than fourth-generation American, as were so many of the "old" Hispanic families of New Mexico. Besides, Mass was celebrated at San Miguel in Latin in those pre–Vatican II decades. Years later Alphonse would recall his training as an altar boy under the guidance of a much-loved pastor, Father Placido Lanz, OAR.[1] The religious among the Augustinian Recollects who served at San Miguel remember the smiling, black-haired boy with the thick glasses. He had revealed to various priests his desire to become a religious and a priest. Later on, he would describe what such a desire might be in reference to a vocation. It is contained in a brief text entitled "Why I Became a Recollect Augustinian."

A vocation is quite puzzling to many people, some define it as a summons to a certain station in life, others as a choice. I, as would every religious, aim to define it as a DESIRE, a YEARNING for that station in life. For one cannot faithfully persevere in a vocation by merely being summoned or by choosing it, he must desire it....Thus an aspirant to the Religious Life selects an Order, not for its richness, not for its popularity, but for those qualities that will enable him to fulfill his DESIRES...and that is why I became a RECOLLECT AUGUSTINIAN.[2]

Who can explain the sources of such desires or yearnings? Alphonse's sister, Senaida, remembers him as quiet and somewhat serious, unlike his outgoing twin, Eloy. He manifested his inclination to the priesthood as had so many future priests by playing "priest" in the dress-up play of children. He was, Senaida remembers, "like his mother," never saying "No" to what was asked of him.

Alphonse improved upon his elementary knowledge of liturgical Latin by taking private lessons from Father Maurice Krautkremer, OAR. Another Recollect friar, Father Jim Elmer, coaxed him through the time of trial and doubt—the time of his two eye surgeries, in 1948 and 1949. Under strict medical instructions to rest following the second surgery, Alphonse had to hold his vocational option in abeyance. Father Elmer promised to visit him during his convalescence and, in the meantime, wrote hopefully to his religious superiors that San Miguel's faithful altar boy would be a "promising prospect."[3]

In the meantime, Alphonse did not allow himself to sit on the sidelines or use his handicap as an excuse for inactivity. He continued his studies at Manual Arts High School in Los Angeles, graduating with honors. But his heart was dedicated to the parish where he followed in the footsteps of his mentor, Eddie Calderon, as the leader of the altar boys and active promoter of the Altar Boys' Club of San Miguel. Beyond the parish, he was an active participant in the Watts Community House with the Catholic Youth Organization (CYO), where he served as discussion leader for the Forum Club, an outgrowth of the diocesan CYO. Not surprisingly, he even came to be a drama director of a one-act play, *In a Doctor's Office,* presented by the local troupe in the Watts Community Center. At the same center, he would serve as president of the CYO Chi Rho Club, an early model of his future dedication to youth and his appreciation for the community-building potential to be found among the young. No doubt he enjoyed the support and encouragement of his CYO companions as he made the decision at the age of twenty to join the Augustinian Recollect religious family to which he had become so attached in the parish of San Miguel. He had kept this decision to himself until the last minute.

Like a Grain of Incense

In the summer of 1950, the preliminaries for Alphonse's entrance into the novitiate of the Augustinian Recollects had been attended to. These included his own formal request, the consent of his parents, academic records, letters of recommendation, and the testimonial letters of the local bishops. The novitiate, a year of initial probation required by church law, was to take place in what was then known as St. Augustine Mission Seminary, in Kansas City, Kansas, a mid-continent removed from the warmth and sun of Southern California.

The religious of the Order of Augustinian Recollects had come to the United States from Spain and Colombia in the early decades of the twentieth century with the intention of serving the growing Catholic Church of the Northern Hemisphere.

They brought with them more than three centuries of missionary experience and a language that was to have increasing importance in the church apostolate in the United States as the Hispanic migration northward evolved throughout the century.

In addition to the task of evangelization, the Augustinian Recollects preserved a way of life with a decidedly communitarian character derived from the *Rule of St. Augustine*. The monastic characteristics were especially applied during the novitiate and the subsequent years of formation. Prior to the reforms and changes introduced by Vatican II, the year of novitiate was governed by the norms of the order's constitution and a book called the *Ceremonial,* written in Latin and carefully studied by the novices. Bells called the novices to prayer, to work, to recreation, and to times of silence, a tight schedule for a well-ordered life. Practices emphasizing humility, obedience, and self-giving constituted the threads of the fabric of the Augustinian Recollect way of life. Alphonse Gallegos adapted beautifully to the Recollect family. He received the black habit of the Augustinian tradition on September 2, 1950, upon entering the novitiate, and made his first profession of the vows of poverty, chastity, and obedience as a religious a day and a year later, on September 3, 1951. As might have been expected, he selected Saint Joseph as his particular patron. The next three years at the Mission Seminary or the Monastery of St. Augustine, as it was more popularly known, would be dedicated to the study of philosophy and the liberal arts.

Years later, as master of novices in the same monastery, between 1967 and 1969, Alphonse diligently applied what he had learned and reflected on at length to a document that he prepared on "Novitiate Training in a Time of Change."[4] Fully cognizant of the need for change and adaptation in the wake of Vatican II and the changes in society, he demonstrates his awareness of the requirements of updating. He retains in this document, however, the core values of self-giving, the spirit of sacrifice and prayer, and love for the community as essential elements of a novitiate experience. He had summarized these aspects of religious life in his earlier mentioned description of his vocation. "He, [the candidate for religious life], like a grain of incense placed upon the burning coals of the censor to achieve its end, must likewise, to attain his goal, be placed upon the coals of training and sacrifice that a Religious Vocation demands of him."[5]

From Mid-America to the Cosmopolitan East

Mobility has long been a characteristic of mendicant communities. The monasticism of the Augustinian Recollects is of the mendicant variety, with community life as the springboard to the apostolate in the itinerant tradition. A move was in order for Brother Alphonse following his profession of solemn vows. The word *solemn* indicates the seriousness of the commitment that a religious undertakes when, upon completion of his three years of temporal profession and acceptance by the community, he promises lifelong fidelity to the vowed life. The young man from San Miguel Parish in Watts made such a promise on September 3, 1954, in the Kansas City monastery. In the case of this candidate from one of the order's parishes, there had been no doubt in the minds of the local religious responsible for judging the aptitude of the candidates for so awesome a pledge. His observance of the three vows during the probationary period was "exemplary" in the opinion of his superiors. With keen perception, they had discovered a quality in Alphonse that prophetically anticipated what would be the outstanding characteristic of his more than forty years in the Lord's service. His superiors made note of this in the following remarks found in the chapter notes of the Kansas City monastery:

Perhaps Frater Alphonse's greatest virtue is his good will. He seems never to have been asked to do, prepare or make anything that he did not receive the request with an abundance of good will and fulfill it to the best of his ability.[6]

By a unanimous vote, he had been approved for this perpetual commitment to religious life. He generously renounced all properties and all rights to future personal possession of the same, a vow he would maintain even after his ascension to the episcopacy. In the midst of such a promising prediction, however, there were shadows. His "eyes are poor," the report continues, a condition that apparently accounted in large part for a comment concerning his "academic deficiency."

Alphonse's history of a severe myopic handicap would accompany him to Tagaste Monastery in Suffern, New York, where he was to begin the theological studies necessary for the priesthood. The damaged eyes began to show signs of additional deterioration and the threat of retinal detachment. The interested physician of the earlier surgeries, Dr. Blasdel of Los Angeles, wrote to Alphonse in a consoling tone, while at the same time reminding him that "being born a very highly near-sighted individual your eyes are much more subject to retinal detachment than would another person's eyes."[7] In the same letter, the doctor strongly advises the young seminarian to avoid strenuous occupations and sports. No doubt, Alphonse's vision problems identified him as a "handicapped" person.

How much would this handicap of vision deficiency influence his powerful desire to be a priest and to serve faithfully the people of God? What might be an insurmountable handicap for someone engaged in a life of study and academic preparation for the priesthood seemed to be for him a further incentive to persevere. His equating of the offering of self to God, with the burning of a grain of incense in the coals of the censor, became a reality. He sought no special treatment nor privileges but lived the seminarian routine of study with the cheerful obedience of always. Due to his limited vision, he was dispensed from reading the Divine Office in common, an essential practice in the mendicant community, but he would join the community at all of the appointed times and would pray the rosary as a substitute for the Breviary. His devotion to the Blessed Virgin Mary was intense and loving.

Doubts about a
Visually Handicapped Priest

As the time for ordination to the priesthood approached, however, serious doubts arose in the minds of his superiors concerning the limitations that Alphonse's handicap had imposed upon his studies. The anguish suffered by the religious summoned to pass judgment on his academic suitability for the priesthood surfaces in the chapter report of January 18, 1958.[8]

> Father Alphonse Gallegos of St. Joseph due to his deficient eyes and [being] unable to study, the chapter convened that he, after being ordained should attend classes for two or three years until he acquires sufficient knowledge to hear confessions properly; after this recommendation he was approved unanimously, (8 white).

As the date of ordination approached, however, doubts were expressed by some of the capitulars (that is, the professed religious appointed to vote on such questions according to canon law and the order's constitutions) concerning the canonical validity of the previous vote. Does this visual handicap constitute an impediment to ordination to the priesthood? The chapter book notes that there was a long discussion on the question, and the vote taken on May 16, 1958, was four white and four black, that is, four in favor of his ordination and four opposed or doubtful.[9] The question was referred to the prior provincial who, upon consultation with the provincial council, dispensed any dubious irregularity that may have been incurred in the previous unanimous vote in favor of Alphonse's suitability for priestly ordination.

Tenacity, constancy, and love for his vocation helped to advance Alphonse to the foot of the altar, which he ascended on May 24, 1958, the day of his ordination to the priesthood at the hands of the consecrating bishop, Most Rev. James H. Griffiths, auxiliary bishop of the Archdiocese of New York. Ordination took place at Tagaste Monastery, the major seminary of the Augustinian Recollects in the United States. He celebrated his first Solemn High Mass in San Miguel Parish on June 8, 1958. He would return to the parish two years later to assist at the bedside of his dying mother, Caciana, whose death was recorded in the parish journal as a "holy and beautiful death."[10]

CHAPTER 3

Preaching the Word

The village of Suffern, New York, where Tagaste is located, would become the area of Father Al's priestly apostolate for the next eight years. His was the welcoming, smiling face that greeted visitors at the front door of the old building overlooking the Ramapo Mountains. His manner of speech, always polite, was that of a teacher of English, clear and precise.

His multiple duties as a newly ordained priest included chaplaincy at numerous convents of religious sisters in the area as well as at Good Samaritan Hospital, located directly across the street from Tagaste. Weekend assistance at the local parishes was a regular part of his initiation to life as, in the words of Saint Augustine, a "dispenser of Word and Sacrament." Not to be forgotten was his assistance to the Blind Players, an organization dedicated to providing summer vacation facilities for the visually handicapped. Part of his interest in this organization included his own efforts to learn Braille. During these years, Tagaste was also the host to the first Cursillos de Cristiandad for the Spanish-speaking of the Archdiocese of New York.

His troubles with his eyes, however, continued to interrupt his total immersion in the apostolate. He was now under the care of the famed Dr. Ramón Castroviejo, who, in an early interview with Alphonse, at the time still a seminarian, expressed surprise that a person with such a severe visual handicap should seek such a profession as the Catholic priesthood, so demanding in terms of study and reading.

In part, the long stay and more sedentary life at Tagaste was a protective, conservative decision of his superiors, unwilling as they were to risk his delicate vision with more taxing assignments. As so often happens, those who do not have such handicaps can be overprotective and not recognize the incredible compensatory power of the will in someone who knows what it is to live in the shadows and blurriness of damaged vision. Father Alphonse did not want special treatment; he even managed to learn how to drive an automobile, to the surprise and terror of his companions. In a sense, this priest-greeter at the monastery, much loved for his gentleness, good humor, and genuine love for people as well as enthusiasm for the gospel, was what might be called a "late bloomer."

"Be Good Alfonso and God Bless You"

The period immediately following his ordination to the priesthood was not without its trials. In 1958, Alphonse underwent a successful operation to correct a retinal detachment in the right eye. In the other eye, however, the situation was less optimistic. Dr. Castroviejo reported that "in the left eye with vision of only light perception, he is affected with total retinal detachment, which cannot be improved neither by medication nor surgery."[1] It appears that the retina of the left eye had atrophied.

In the midst of these procedures and treatments, which took place in the first two years of his priestly ministry, he received the support of the Recollect community and his family. Some letters from his mother, Caciana, written during this period have been conserved. She was not herself in good health due to a debilitating cardiac deficiency. The letters are gems of a simple, uncomplaining piety, in which she informs her son of her condition but more so of the gratitude she owed to God and a loving family for so much help and concern. The profound love that characterized the marriage of José and Caciana is captured in a beautiful quote from a letter written on May 2, 1960.

> The girls are sure taking care of me they come and clean the house for me. Poor Daddy he helps too. He feels so bad when I am sick. I've been praying to the Blessed Mother, St. Joseph and the Sacred Heart of Jesus to get me well. I know Daddy needs me and I need him.[2]

Caciana reminded her son of the "nice people" of the parish of San Miguel who always asked for him. And, of course, she reported on the successful remembrance of the twenty-fifth anniversary of the "Saint Joseph Wake"[3] celebrated that same year of 1960 with the family friends and neighbors in attendance. Each of these letters ends with some simple advice to a priest son: "Be good Alfonso and God bless you." It would be the last celebration of Saint Joseph's feast for Caciana, who went to her heavenly reward on June 10, 1960, to be followed by her beloved husband, José, eleven years later on June 10, 1971.

Father Alphonse Meets the "Me" Generation

The first change in the long period of ministry on behalf of the Tagaste community came in the summer of 1966, when the still-young Father Gallegos was chosen by the provincial and provincial council to become prefect of the professed students at the Monastery of St. Augustine in Kansas City, Kansas, the scene of his own novitiate and early years of formation as an Augustinian Recollect. Upon the resignation of the master of novices for reasons of health, Father Alphonse took over as master of novices. During his assignment as master of novices, a very responsible position, he confronted a mentality among the young candidates quite different from what had been the pre-Vatican II piety of his own generation. The tensions in the houses of formation were intense in the late '60s, as communities began to rewrite constitutions and to respond to the requirements of the Second Vatican Council concerning both a return to the basic charism of the congregation and an appropriate adaptation to the changing times. Everything was questioned, and a continual pressure for experimentation seemed to be the order of the day. The candidates were more skeptical, more self-conscious of their individuality, more questioning of tradition and authority. The situation was certainly a challenge to a man of ready obedience and genuine humility.

But, Father Alphonse did not close the door to the new generation; his passionate concern for youth, so evident in his future ministries as pastor and bishop, was tested and intensified in the difficult years during which he served as master of novices. He was known by his subjects to be strict yet fair, prayerful yet always cheerful. Some saw in him an authority figure at a time when all authority roles were being questioned. It was not an easy time for a religious who had spoken about "a grain of incense" on the altar of sacrifice.

Time for a Personal Renewal

These very qualities of manly piety and unfailing charity kept him in the area of formation after his three years as director of the novitiate. In the summer of 1969, he returned to Tagaste as assistant prior and prefect of the theologians, to which was added the job as full-time chaplain at the Sisters of Charity Good Samaritan Hospital. But, it was not just a repetition of his earlier years at Tagaste. Something of a major change occurred in Alphonse's life at this juncture. He seemed to want to break out of the inhibiting limitations of his chronic battle with his vision handicap. There was a new "can do" decisiveness that led him to seek permission to advance his own education, which, due to his eye problems, had been spotty and irregular. Permission was granted, and he enrolled in St. Thomas Aquinas College in Sparkill, New York, an institution of the Dominican Sisters located not far from Suffern. He joined a group of young students attending night school and commuted with them to evening classes. To this day, his commuter companions remember his cheerful companionship. He won his Bachelor of Science degree in psychology in June 1970 and, encouraged by this success, accepted a new challenge by enlisting in the master's degree program in counseling at St. John's University, Jamaica, New York. To accomplish the same, he undertook the daunting challenge of commuting by bus, train, and subway from semi-rural Suffern to the city campus of the university. Again, a triumph! He received his master's degree in June 1972. These victories over his handicap and this decisive embracing of an open future would prove to be of major consequence in the following years of Father Gallegos's response to the vocation that he had so ardently desired.

CHAPTER 4

Watts Is "Out of Control"

The Return of the Native Son

It is customary among religious orders to hold assemblies, which are called "chapters," every three years or more, to select superiors and define the programs of the congregation. Following the provincial chapter of 1972, which was held in Kansas City, Father Alphonse was given his first parish assignment after fourteen years of ministry in the houses of formation of the Province of St. Augustine. He was appointed pastor of his home parish, the Church of San Miguel in Watts. As was to be expected, he acceded to the decision of his superiors without hesitation, although he had a later-expressed concern about the return of the native son to his home grounds: the biblical adage about the prophet not being accepted in his own country. Whatever fear he might have had about his acceptance by the parishioners of San Miguel or his effectiveness as prophet soon vanished. From the day on which he assumed the pastorate and made his profession of faith—August 2, 1972—he initiated a pastoral practice that was definitely marked by three constants: his love for children, his concern for the youth, and his passion for education.

Watts had been the center of national interest during the violent riots that rocked the neighborhood and the city of Los

Angeles during the summer of 1965. The racial mix in this neighborhood of poverty consisted of an African American majority and a longtime Mexican American minority. Many of the Mexican American families, friends and neighbors of the Gallegos family, had moved on to other areas of the city as their fortunes improved. Watts remained, however, a magnet for the new arrivals and undocumented immigrants from Mexico and Latin America. The riots were expressions of an accumulation of grievances that had surfaced during those years of turmoil and struggle in the name of human and civil rights for all. The comment of the religious at the parish during the time of the riots was that matters are "out of control in Watts, the central section of the district is in flames."[1] After the destruction and street violence, order was restored to the barrio, but a sense of insecurity remained. It was one of those neighborhoods into which a nonresident did not enter, especially after dark. The rise and threatening presence of the gangs contributed to the sense of social unease and stress.

Perhaps the social environment of the Watts parish was best summarized in the comments made by the house chronicler in the following text taken from the *Libro de cosas notables* for Christmas 1971, the year before Father Alphonse arrived as pastor.

> Mid-Night Mass, *Misa de Gallo*. It is a challenge to have any kind of service at night in our church but we had Mid-Night Mass this Christmas and every Christmas at least since 1966. We had a good number of people and nothing bad or deplorable happened that night as far as I know. Batteries from cars are often stolen and sometimes the cars are stolen and set on fire. What is worse yet, men and women are beaten up and robbed in the street and [they] break into their homes stealing all they can. This happened here in Watts any time and all the time during the day and at night. They have broken in

20

quite a few times in our school and stolen typewriters and television sets and other things. About two years ago the silent alarm system was installed in the school to protect it from thieves getting inside the school on weekends and other times. But still they have managed somehow to brake [sp.] inside the school two different times and ransacked the class rooms. With all these things going on, this is not *Dante's Inferno* but *Watts Inferno.*[2]

It was in this context of poverty, fear, and suspicion that Father Alphonse Gallegos began his pastorate, promising in a letter to his provincial to do his "best in trying to meet the needs of the people and to work for the glory of God in re-vitalizing the spiritual element of the community."[3] Contained within this promise are three key goals that would govern the apostolic thrust of the new pastor. These are (1) the needs of the people, multiple, material as well as spiritual; (2) revitalization of the spiritual element, that is, the family and potential lay leadership; (3) working for the glory of God, that is, the forgetting of self and imitating the ways of Christ in daily celebration and ministry.

The People and Their Needs

Poverty has many faces and is a term that can be aptly applied to many human situations of depravity and helplessness. What comes first to mind is the lack of material resources, the economic means wherewith to sustain a life of minimum security in the basic areas of nourishment, housing, and health. A church parish has limited means with which to respond to these needs; it can mainly serve as a coordinating or participating figure with the various larger philanthropic or civil agencies. These areas were to be studied in detail in a special report sponsored by and prepared for the Augustinian Recollects by the Center for Applied Research in the Apostolate (C.A.R.A.).[4] But, there is another area of poverty, which is that which constitutes the "culture of poverty," the absence or lack of the cultural means and skills with which to confront life in the complicated urban setting of one of America's largest cities. It is not surprising, therefore, that Father Alphonse would make education and the parish school top priorities in his parish plan.

"Education for a Better Community" was the underlying theme of a "School Philosophy" that was initiated by the new pastor upon his return to Watts. Brother Michael Stechmann, an Augustinian Recollect teacher who worked side by side with the future bishop, remarked very perceptively in a letter to an admirer of Bishop Gallegos that

> he [A.G.] helped to stress with the faculty, parents, students and parishioners that one of the most primary services that we can give to the community is to educate our students in such a way as to form them into valuable assets, capable of rendering beneficial services and edifying and upgrading the local community.[5]

Few documents concerning Alphonse Gallegos are as accurate and convincing as this heartfelt letter written by a companion who daily witnessed how his pastor cheerfully lived out the gospel values that he professed.

Father Al made it his daily practice to greet the children at the beginning of the school day and to meet them again in the afternoon as they were returning home. A parent who was upset by the possible transfer of Father Alphonse from San Miguel to another parish summarized the magnetism of his pastor's apostolate to the children and, as is evident, to the families, stating that "every time my children (come) from school or Sunday Mass, telling me Father Gallegos shook my hand, told me a joke or he was talking to us." The same letter addressed to Father's superiors contained a message from the heart of the writer; his pastor had been a "God-given gift to His children, people and community."[6]

In addition to the personal pastoral approach to the children, Father Gallegos had guided his teaching community toward a school philosophy well-articulated in the San Miguel Elementary School Self-Evaluation document formally prepared in April 1975. The pastor and his staff realistically paid attention to the conditions of the families in the neighborhood, whose annual earnings, in many cases, were well below the poverty level. To counter the negative economic data, the school policy was expressed in the previously mentioned theme of "Education for a Better Community," emphasizing "the actualization that each child realizes and respects his dignity as a person, understands and takes pride in his cultural heritage, and grasps an authentic relationship with his God."[7] The enrollment had reached 350 students.

The community-based school program was such a success that in 1977, five years after his appointment to the parish, he could write to the chancery of the Archdiocese of Los Angeles requesting that the financial subsidy granted to the parish be discontinued.[8] Both facts, the rise of student enrollment and successful fund-raising, speak of a remarkable change in a neighborhood condemned to decay and social chaos. The decision to forego funding, however, would prove to be controversial for future pastors of San Miguel Parish who did not have the same access to funding sources that had become available to Father Alphonse as a native son of the Los Angeles and the Watts communities. What was important to the pastor, however, was his desire to move this underprivileged community toward a sense of pride in freeing itself from dependence on funding from the archdiocese. Community building has much to do with the image that the people of the area have of themselves, and Father Gallegos sought to create a positive self-awareness in this barrio served by the parish of San Miguel.

Chaplain to the "Low-Riders"

The very active ministry of the future bishop to the children, the families, and the youth of Watts had the backing of the religious community in which he had made his profession as an Augustinian Recollect. Father Al was accompanied and supported by other priests and brothers of the community who joined with him in prayer, the daily Eucharist, and the parish ministries. As a local superior, he knew how to share ideas, work, and projects. They also shared the "table of the poor" in an atmosphere of fraternity and good humor. All of the religious who had known or lived with Alphonse were struck by his undying optimism and unfailing cheerfulness. Every day with Al began as a "beautiful morning." His smile was contagious and extended to all, the mendicant illegal at the rectory door, the hostile environments of Watts's broken homes, and even to the noisy "low-riders"[9] who dominated the Friday and Saturday nights of the inner-city barrios. To be sure, he was a weekend regular at their street-corner gatherings, blessing the highly decorated cars, inviting the youth to church, and encouraging them to think about an education.

Upon his appointment as auxiliary bishop of the Diocese of Sacramento, he stated in a press release (September 1, 1981) that "I would like very much to be a Bishop of the youth and for the youth." A summary of his approach to the young of Watts is contained in the following comment to a journalist.

> During my six years in Watts, I visited youth in their homes, met with them on street corner and the basketball court, invited them to the rectory, had programs for them in the parish hall and took them to colleges and universities. We saw 27 young men and women graduate from college. Before, standing on the street corner, they felt the world had nothing to offer—until they discovered that they had something to offer the world.[10]

This emphasis on personal and community upgrading through education was reflected in his own advancement in the academic ranks when he attained another master's degree in religious studies and education at Los Angeles's Loyola-Marymount University while serving as pastor of San Miguel.

One of the pioneer projects for the spiritual and religious formation of the Hispanics of the Archdiocese of Los Angeles went well beyond the parish boundaries. In close collaboration with the archbishop, Cardinal Timothy Manning, and the archdiocesan offices, Father Alphonse helped to establish one of the first permanent diaconate programs in the country for the Spanish-speaking. Such gestures reveal the concept of "church" that guided San Miguel's pastor. He thought in terms of a parish not as an isolated community but as a living cell in the Body of Christ, the universal church.

Watts, "Impoverished but Not Sad"

The chronicles of San Miguel Parish during the six years of Father Gallegos's pastorate, 1972-1978, provide a virtually day-to-day record of the pastoral approach followed by Father Alphonse and his Augustinian Recollect companions from the date of his arrival at the parish, August 26, 1972. After meeting with the archbishop, Cardinal Manning, and Bishop John Ward, vicar general and regional bishop, Father Alphonse invited the youth of the area to reactivate the Catholic Youth Organization, the CYO of his young days in Watts. By October, the first parish council was formed to fulfill the requirements of post-Vatican II canon law. It was to provide advice and support in the following six areas of interest: (1) education, (2) social affairs, (3) liturgy and music, (4) youth, (5) properties, and (6) finance.

Efforts were made by the pastor to enlist the support of family and former parishioners, with very positive results. Certainly, it was a "conscience-raising" strategy, whereby those who had advanced socially and economically were called upon to remember those who were "left behind" in poverty and those who had recently arrived in search of a better life. For many of the old-timers, Watts had drastically changed. Gangs and gang warfare, as well as the intrusion of drugs and drug dealers, had made living in Watts a matter of last resort. Recognizing these realities, Father Gallegos and his team, which included the Augustinian Recollect priests and brothers who formed the religious community, the Sisters of the Love of God who served in the school, and the lay volunteers, reached out to a wider constituency for support. Again, Father Gallegos's concept of the "church as one," which was the key notion behind his labor as auxiliary bishop of the Sacramento Diocese, emphasized the notion of a shared responsibility of the more affluent in caring for the less fortunate and their neighborhoods. It was realized in Watts when former parishioners responded to the pastor's call for assistance.

One sector that began to assist was organized labor. Father Alphonse was invited to speak at various union functions, bringing to the attention of these national advocates of social justice the abysmal conditions of the unprotected elements of inner-city populations that had been "left behind" in spite of the broad economic advances of the American worker. He did not hesitate to communicate with the city government and the police agencies in his struggle on behalf of the local population for various aid programs and better police protection. Nor was the fabled Hollywood beyond his pleas for his flock, and there was, from time to time, generous support from persons in the entertainment industry.

The strong emphasis given to family and community, two interdependent social entities upon which the security and peace of a neighborhood or city depend, was evident in the promotion of family prayer, especially the rosary, the organization of the Living Rosary in the various city blocks surrounding the parish, and the careful preparation of the liturgies of Sunday and feast days. In addition to these spiritual experiences of community, the pastor and his associates used every opportunity to bring people together in social settings, enabling them to become acquainted and to overcome the fears that had kept people apart and isolated.

One rather interesting happening was the annual transformation of the quintessential American celebration of Thanksgiving into a parish event. The significance of Thanksgiving, given its peculiar Anglo-American origin, is not easily grasped by a newcomer to the United States. The San Miguel pastoral team turned the holiday into a parish banquet to which all were invited. The chronicles speak of 300 to 500 people in attendance at the parish hall, where the pastor, the sisters, the brothers, and the volunteers served the standard American turkey to the huge gathering.

Typically, Father Al spent Christmas and Easter visiting homes and families in the parish neighborhood. The neighborhood itself was in the process of transformation. The very youth who had painted graffiti on the walls of the parish buildings were challenged to replace the violent pictures with creative works of spiritual significance. These same young people, some of whom had been associated with gangs and drugs, were encouraged to cooperate in teaching summer school or tutoring the younger children and to assist in the adult education programs conducted throughout the year. No group was excluded. Father Javier Iturri, OAR, veteran missionary and senior priest, served as coordinator of the seniors.

These, indeed, were exciting years for Father Alphonse Gallegos, who seemed to find time for everything and for everyone. The experience of serving as shepherd of souls in the often violent and conflictive barrio of Watts would later serve him as a model for his future role as auxiliary bishop of Sacramento, a not-even-thought-of possibility when, on June 30, 1978, he received notice of his transfer to Cristo Rey Parish in Glendale.

The Glory of God

As a seminarian, it was noted that Brother Alphonse "always gave the greater part of his time to study and the reading of spiritual and devotional works."[11] His "desire to give himself wholly to God," as was expressed in his statement explaining his vocation, "Why I Became a Recollect Augustinian," was firmly based upon a life of prayer. Due to his vision deficiency, he was allowed to substitute the recitation of the Holy Rosary for the reading of the Divine Office but, not for this privilege, did he absent himself from assisting at community prayer. "He seems never to have absented himself from community acts without sufficient reason"[12] is the way his superiors described his attention to the prayer life of the community.

These practices supported his dedication to the liturgy and community prayers in the parish. On the eve of his departure from San Miguel to assume the pastorate of Cristo Rey Church in Glendale, his parish council summarized very well his impact on the spiritual life of that often troubled neighborhood of Watts. "It is a very rare occasion," they wrote, "that anyone can take hold of a community that is spiritually dying and with the grace of God make it reborn through that person's faith in Our Lord and love for his people."[13]

Cardinal Manning seconded the concern of the parishioners of San Miguel in a letter to the prior general of the Order of Augustinian Recollects. "Father Gallegos is a shepherd dearly loved by his people, intensely pastoral in his concerns....[He is] an appointee to our Senate of Priests and deeply involved in the Permanent Diaconate Program."[14] Father Gallegos had found that God was present in Watts in spite of the dehumanizing poverty and criminality. He had another way of looking at reality, which, perhaps, can only be seen with the "eyes of the heart," a biblical expression much loved by Saint Augustine and a graced privilege reserved for the prophets. Cardinal Roger Mahony, successor to Cardinal Manning in the Archdiocese of Los Angeles, recalled in his homily at the funeral Mass for Bishop Gallegos that

> about three years after his appointment as pastor, Father Gallegos reflected on the need for joy as an instrument of God's grace: Watts, noted the future bishop, is an impoverished area, but not a sad area. There is a lot of spirit, a lot of hope. It is a very happy community in spite of everything.[15]

CHAPTER 5

A Call to a Wider Ministry

Cristo Rey and the California Catholic Conference

The prior general of the Augustinian Recollects had replied to Cardinal Manning's concern about the possibility of losing the services of Father Gallegos in the Los Angeles Archdiocese by stating the two consecutive three-year terms as a religious superior or pastor was the constitutional norm of the order. He reassured him at the same time that the newly to-be-elected prior provincial and council would take into consideration the cardinal's request.[1]

As a result of the provincial chapter of 1978, Father Gallegos was not removed from the Los Angeles Archdiocese but was named pastor of Cristo Rey Parish in the Glendale section of Los Angeles County. The transfer was official as of July 16, 1978. Cristo Rey is a small parish, territorially speaking. It was founded and built by the Mexican American population of the vicinity in cooperation with the Augustinian Recollect religious. Although it had less of a reputation for violence than did Watts, Glendale presented a similar pastoral situation. There was a need to respond to the spiritual and devotional customs of an older, more settled, traditional, and largely Mexican population, with their Americanized children and grandchildren, as well as to reach out to the never-abating immigration of Latin Americans, both legal and illegal. It did not take long for Father Alphonse to win the hearts of his parishioners.

Within a year of his transfer to Watts, however, Father Gallegos's reputation had come to the attention of the California bishops who had recently established a Division of Hispanic Affairs under the auspices of the California Catholic Conference, the statewide consortium of bishops. The post of director for the new division was offered to Father Gallegos, who, in his customary manner, placed the matter in the hands of his superiors both diocesan and religious. There was some reluctance on the part of both. Cardinal Manning felt the loss of a diocesan leader among the Hispanics and a good friend, who would now be relocated to Sacramento, the headquarters of the California Catholic Conference. A similar sadness within joy of seeing a brother religious recognized in such a singular fashion by the bishops of California was a natural reaction among the Recollects to his separation from their normal life in community.

The establishment of a Division of Hispanic Affairs for Region XI by the California Catholic Conference in 1979 was a response to the pressing need on the part of the church in California to address the ever-increasing importance of the Spanish-speaking population in the Golden State. "Father Gallegos appeared to be the most suitable" among the candidates for the position of director "when the California Catholic Conference finally was in a position to establish a Division of Hispanic Affairs." Thus wrote the auxiliary bishop of Los Angeles, Bishop John Ward, who added to his comments that he had taught catechism to the new director when, as a young priest and seminarian, he had served in the Watts area.[2]

The Hispanic presence in California is both historic and contemporary. The early settlement and development of the vast territory as part of the Spanish Empire had endowed it with the colonial culture of the missions and civic centers of soldiers, merchants, and ranchers who gave an identity to the state still present in the names of towns, cities, and highways. More sociologically acute, however, has been the continuing migration of Spanish-speaking, especially but not exclusively Mexican, people into the state throughout the twentieth and into the twenty-first centuries. Beginning with the *Cristeros,* those Catholics escaping from the religious persecution in Mexico in the 1920s and 1930s, the immigration trend continued, with thousands of workers and farm laborers moving north to seek new opportunities and economic support for their families. Although the California church had responded to the phenomenon on a local level, the evident and overwhelming presence of this new population, often quite mobile, called for a concerted, interdiocesan effort to care for the uprooted and frequently economically deprived Hispanic arrivals.

A very detailed job description had been prepared for the new director upon his transfer to the offices of the California Catholic Conference in Sacramento. The Region XI Conference of Spanish-Speaking (RECOSS) had been created as the bishops' coordinating instrument for the Hispanic apostolate. The Division of Hispanic Affairs, to be directed by Father Gallegos, was charged with providing reliable information of a statistical nature as well as reports on resources such as personnel and pastoral and educational programs for Region XI (RECOSS). There was also a list of unrealized projects, such as the creation of a media outreach to the Spanish-speaking, catechetical materials, and formation programs for the laity. The director was also to maintain liaison with the national secretariat for the Spanish-speaking of the American Bishops' Conference, the local offices for Hispanic Ministry, as well as advising on legislative matters under consideration by the state government with regard to the Spanish-speaking. Such was the web of obligations and opportunities that awaited the myopic visionary as he began his journey north from Glendale to his new assignment. He writes in his personal journal, which he apparently started upon the occasion of his separation from his religious family for the first time since he entered the Monastery of St. Augustine in Kansas City, Kansas, in the summer of 1950:

> Left Cristo Rey parish to assume my duties as Director of the Division of Hispanic Affairs with the California Catholic Conference. This new office makes me responsible to 21 bishops and 11 dioceses....Giving thanks to Almighty God for having allowed me to be part of Cristo Rey parish [and] San Miguel parish, I leave for San Francisco by car to attend my first official meeting with the Bishops from Region XI.[3]

A Friar's Journal

It has been an ancient tradition among religious communities of a monastic character to maintain a house history or record of "Notable Events." As Father Alphonse left Los Angeles to enter into a new world of pastoral work on a broad scale within the framework of offices, committees, and extensive outreach, he kept in touch with the tradition of the house journal. On a daily basis for the next three years, he maintained a handwritten diary that, in keeping with the community tradition, he would eventually submit to his religious superior, the prior provincial, for inspection and approval. Although now experiencing the more independent lifestyle of the diocesan clergy, Father Al maintained strong ties to the community with which he was deeply attached by reason of his religious consecration and fraternal sentiments.

His day-by-day recording of events, begun on October 1, 1979, reveals a readiness on his part to assume his new duties with energy and with that particular air of confidence and tenacity that he had cultivated in his long battle with his handicap of seriously impaired vision. He had come to a decision early on that he did not want to be assigned or judged on the basis of his handicap but, rather, that he be considered as one more priest and religious available for assignment where needed. He was now full time at the service of the bishops, the priests, the religious, and the laity of California in the huge and complicated challenge of aiding an institution, the Catholic Church of California, reach out to the multifaceted phenomenon of the Hispanic presence.

The contents of the journal reveal a fast-paced initiation and high-level insertion into a process of pastoral planning on behalf of the apostolate to the Hispanic populations of the state of California. He refers to the work of coordinating with other agencies of the eleven dioceses of the Golden State as well as maintaining communications with the national offices of the United States Bishops' Conference relative to the needs of the Hispanics and the resources available to meet such needs. Another level of communications would be that of sharing data and resources with the bishops of neighboring Mexico.

After a round of introductions to the personnel of the Office of the California Catholic Conference, he writes, "I began my work as Director of the Division of Hispanic Affairs."[4] What follows is the report, day by day, of a demanding schedule of meetings and travels that would carry him to a wide-ranging involvement in the various diocesan organizations both already established or in the process of coming into existence. The objectives of these various alphabetized entities were the areas of concern of the rapidly growing and needful Hispanic populations of California. Personal contact with those who were responsible for the organizational aspects of statewide pastoral planning was the task of the new director of the Hispanic Affairs Office. Although he dearly missed the daily pastoral life of the parish, he gave himself to the new task with the same affable spirit that was his hallmark as a parish priest.

This new engagement with the administrative structures of the Bishops' Conference did not keep him totally separated from the local pastoral scene. On October 3, 1979, he took up temporary residence in Holy Spirit Parish, moving on October 13 to the parish of St. Rose, located at Franklin Boulevard and 38th Street in Sacramento, where he would serve as an associate to the legendary Monsignor Edward J. Kavanagh, longtime pastor of this large inner-city parish. Although his pastoral activity at the local level would be necessarily limited, it would be a continuation of the practices he had so successfully employed in Watts as the Friday night chaplain to the "low-riders."

"Father Gallegos Is Taking It to the Streets"

High on the list of the pastoral priorities of the Bishops' Conference was the plight of the undocumented immigrant, so often subject to economic exploitation and so often deprived of the minimal conditions for decent and humane living. One of Father Alphonse's first assignments was to serve as executive secretary of a special committee of American and Mexican bishops formed to address the issue of the undocumented. His outreach to the undocumented migrant was not simply a theoretical concern but a reality that he chose to confront by direct contact. With the newly installed ordinary of Sacramento, Bishop Francis Quinn (February 18, 1980), former auxiliary bishop of the Archdiocese of San Francisco, he engaged in a series of pastoral visits to several large farming communities or camps of migrant workers and their families in order to assess the needs and the plight of the migrant laborer. Parallel to obtaining firsthand information concerning these often infra-human living conditions, there was a strong effort on the part of the new director of Hispanic affairs to plan a common strategy of pastoral care for the migrant, coordinating the approaches of the bishops in both California and Mexico. Father Gallegos remarked that the long-awaited discussion finally took place and "focused on pastoral concerns affecting hundreds of thousands of migrant Catholics on both sides of the border."[5] After what he called the "great experience" of celebrating the Eucharist for the farm laborers and their families in Dixon, California, he met with the governor of California to promote the cause of the migrant.[6]

The issue of the immigrant laborer was, however, far more complicated than a matter of civil status. It was, for Father Gallegos, a question of safeguarding the religious faith and heritage of the Hispanic uprooted from the familiar community of Catholic formation and culture to which he had been accustomed. Evangelization was, thus, a principal area of concern that caused Alphonse to insist upon the need to create a viable and appropriate use of the various means of communication, such as Spanish-language radio and television, in order to reach out to such a dispersed population. In fact, his first major conference to the Region XI Commission for the Spanish-speaking (January 28, 1980) was entitled, "The Spiritual Aspects of Ministry to the Spanish-Speaking."

A prime target group for evangelization in line with Father Gallegos's priorities was the youth. His journal entries include dates set aside for vocation retreats and for gatherings of catechists. He recalls in his journal (July 30, 1981) the day he "met with the Mayor of Sacramento and Bishop Francis Quinn to discuss the need to work with the youth." "We shared ideas," he adds, and, it seems, "both were pleased with my work with the 'low-riders.'" Monsignor Kavanagh, pastor of the parish of St. Rose, remembers that this priest in residence at the parish, Father Al, made Friday and Saturday night visits to the street-corner gatherings of the local Latinos along Franklin Boulevard. Father Al saw something of value in the care and creative artistry with which the "low-riders" embellished their low-slung automobiles: points of encounter and occasions for a blessing or an invitation. A local journalist describes the phenomenon of the priest's nocturnal visits to the "low-riders" as "Father Gallegos is taking it to the streets."[7]

A Mysterious Phone Call

Due to his status as a spokesman for the Hispanics of California, Father Gallegos was in contact with the various national Catholic commissions dealing with issues of interest to this population group. Some of these contacts were also international. Father Gallegos was invited by Pablo Sedillo of the Secretariat of Hispanic Affairs of the National Conference of Catholic Bishops to attend a meeting on "The Church and Labor" sponsored by Catholic labor groups in Caracas, Venezuela. His conference topic was to be "Labor in the Southwest and West of the United States of America."[8] As was his custom when traveling in the United States or abroad, he visited the local Augustinian Recollect ministries and communities if there were any in the region. It so happened that, when he visited "our Church of Our Lady of Guadalupe" in Caracas, he was told by the friars that the bishop of Sacramento had called using the code name of "Howard."[9] Something was in the air, but, apparently, a call back to the number given was a wrong number and a second call to the offices of the California Catholic Conference provided no information relative to the mysterious telephone call. After visiting and celebrating the Eucharist with various Augustinian Recollect communities in Caracas, Alphonse returned to Sacramento via a long twenty-two hours spent on a series of flights and transfers.

On August 26, according to the journal entry, Bishop Quinn called the St. Rose rectory and asked Father Gallegos to meet him at the corner of 11th and I streets in order to prepare for a meeting with the mayor concerning the youth of the city. What took place, however, is best reported in the words of the future auxiliary bishop of Sacramento.

> I met the Bishop at 5:15 p.m. and he immediately told me that His Holiness Pope John Paul II had nominated me to the Episcopacy. I felt humbled and stunned. We talked for some 30 minutes. I frankly asked the Bishop if he really wanted me as his Auxiliary Bishop. He answered that he would be delighted if I would accept. I asked if he would allow me to pray over this serious appointment. He allowed me to spend the night in prayer and asked me to call him at 8:30 the next morning. I spent the night in prayer asking the Holy Spirit to enlighten me to make the right decision and to do the will of God. I asked Our Lady to assist me to be humble and open to the will of her Son. I felt frightened and humbled. My nomination as Auxiliary Bishop of Sacramento, Calif., and Titular Bishop of Sasabe was a complete surprise to me.
>
> Aug. 22. At 8:30 a.m. I called Bishop Francis Quinn to give him my answer. I shared his advice to me: "the Holy Father has chosen you." I never felt the presence of the Holy Spirit as I did this day. For Holy Obedience to our Holy Father and strengthened by the Holy Spirit, I consented to become the Auxiliary Bishop of Sacramento and Titular Bishop of Sasabe. Once I responded to the will of God, a calm came over me. I then went to celebrate the Eucharist in thanksgiving and personal dedication to God and His Church. I was told by Bishop Quinn that a pontifical secret was to be observed until the announcement was made by the Apostolic Delegate in Washington, D.C.[10]

Hispanic Bishop for Sacramento

The silence required by the Holy See with respect to the publication of the news of the elevation of Father Gallegos to the episcopate was broken on September 1, 1981. He recorded in his journal that "the phone rang at 6:30 a.m. It was Bishop Francis Quinn calling to congratulate me and to inform me that my nomination as Bishop was now public."[11] A flood of telephone calls inundated the rectory of St. Rose Parish as callers across the nation congratulated the new prelate, the first Hispanic bishop in the Diocese of Sacramento since 1861. Accompanied by his ordinary, Bishop Quinn, Bishop-Elect Gallegos issued a statement to the press relative to his new position. Expressing gratitude to His Holiness, Pope John Paul II, and to Bishop Quinn, he quickly added his appreciation for the loving support of the priests, religious, and laity of the diocese, of his family and the Augustinian Recollect community. He recognized that the "honor bestowed on me is truly an honor bestowed upon the Hispanic community."[12] True to his pastoral practices as a priest in the barrio, he requested the special assistance of the youth of the diocese and expressed a desire to be "a Bishop of the youth and for the youth."[13] Citing the central theme of the *Rule of St. Augustine,* he concluded with a salute to his Augustinian Recollect heritage: "Above all things, let us love God and our neighbor, for this is the principal precept given to us by God Himself."[14] "Love one another" would be inscribed in the symbolic belt or cincture at the base of his episcopal coat of arms.

The choice of a coat of arms, a long-standing tradition among those clerics raised to the rank of bishop in the Roman Catholic Church, would be just one of the many activities mentioned in the bishop-elect's journal during the months prior to the date set for his ordination to the episcopacy, November 4, 1981, the feast day of Saint Charles Borromeo. He was still director of the Office of Hispanic Affairs for the California Catholic

Conference. Undoubtedly, he was reflecting upon his future role and expressed his priorities in the coat of arms that was designed with the help of heraldic artists and staff companions. On the background of a white shield, one could visualize the snows of the Sierra Mountains, part of the vast panorama of the Sacramento Diocese; a triple-branched nettle tree, a symbol taken from the ancient coat of arms of the Gallegos family; and seven leaves stemming from the tree to represent the seven sacraments. Present too would be a type of carpenter's square honoring the family patron, Saint Joseph, and a gold rose recalling Our Lady of Guadalupe. Not to be left out were two Aztec wings reminiscent of San Miguel, the patron of the church in Watts. All came to rest on the "Love One Another" of Augustinian inspiration.

On the day of the episcopal ordination, Bishop Francis Quinn, principal consecrator and celebrant, was accompanied by the co-consecrators, Archbishop John R. Quinn, Archdiocese of San Francisco, and Archbishop Robert F. Sanchez, Archdiocese of Santa Fe, as well as twenty-four bishops and a large representation of clergy, religious, and laity. A festive spirit was evident in the day-long celebration, which clearly manifested the multicolored ethnicity of California's capital city. The real work, however, for the next ten years—between the joyful events of November 4, 1981, and the tragic accident of October 6, 1991—would be accomplished in a daily spirit of the giving of self to God and to others, as he promised he would do on the day of his first vows as an Augustinian Recollect religious on September, 3, 1951.

Alphonse Gallegos's family (from the top, left to right): Soledad JoJola (grand-mother), Jacob Gallegos (grandfather), Silvester Gallegos (great uncle), Procoio Gallegos (great uncle), John José Gallegos (great grandfather), Refina De Silva (great grandmother), Isabell Gallegos-JoJola (great aunt), Theo JoJola (great grandfather), Jim Gallegos (uncle), Ben Gallegos (uncle), Sara JoJola (aunt).

Alphonse at the time of his high school graduation in 1950.

Alphonse Gallegos had a lifelong interest in music (here pictured as a young seminarian in Kansas City, Kansas).

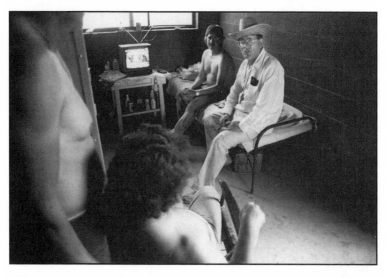

Alphonse Gallegos speaks with farmworkers, whom he visited frequently during his ministry in California.

Bishop Alphonse Gallegos greets Cesar Chavez, founder of the United Farm Workers union.

As bishop, Alphonse Gallegos reached out to all members of the community, Catholic and non-Catholic alike. Here, giving the invocation during a civic function in Sacramento.

Bishop Gallegos's proverbial love for children was always an important part of his ministry.

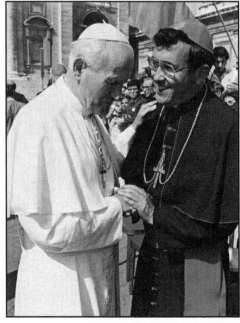

Bishop Gallegos speaks with Pope John Paul II in St. Peter's Square during a visit to Rome.

CHAPTER 6

The Joy of Being Catholic

The Diocese of Sacramento:
A Pastoral Challenge

What lay ahead for the young bishop, just fifty years of age in 1981? Much had been said of the fact that Bishop Gallegos was the first Hispanic bishop to serve the church in Sacramento since 1861, the final year of administration by Archbishop José Sadoc Alemany, Archbishop of San Francisco, whose territorial jurisdiction also included the not-yet-erected Diocese of Sacramento. Certainly, in the intervening century and a half, vast social and demographic changes had taken place. Today, the Diocese of Sacramento covers some 43,000 square miles of land area and serves more than a half a million Catholics in a total population of 3,169,750. The twenty counties in this configuration extend from the urban southern region of the city of Sacramento and environs to the rural farming and logging areas of the north, bordering on the states of Oregon and Nevada. Many ethnic groups are to be found throughout the region, reflecting the multicultural realities of the state of California.

Following the transfer of California from Mexican to North American sovereignty, the church of the fabled missions became the object of ecclesiastical reorganization in which, over the succeeding decades, new dioceses came into existence and a largely Irish and Irish American clergy began to serve the rapidly growing Catholic population fueled by the great migration of Europeans to the United States. The cooperative arrangements between the local dioceses and the Catholic seminaries of Ireland provided a supply of priests energetically dedicated to the founding of parishes and schools. The native Hispanic population, survivors of the older Spanish Mexican colonial times, receded into the background. There was to be, however, a new Hispanic presence growing steadily throughout the twentieth century. Bishop Gallegos's appointment as auxiliary bishop of Sacramento was a recognition of the new demographics and a response to the need for ecclesiastical leadership from within this rapidly growing minority. The new bishop was careful to clarify for the press both his special connection with the Hispanic population and his desire to serve all of the people of the diocese without distinction. "I do see [Hispanics] as a special ministry since I am Hispanic. This does not mean I will not be a pastor to all the people of the diocese."[1] The priest from Watts and an Augustinian Recollect religious was not a complete stranger to the Sacramento clergy, since he had been at the California Catholic Conference office for two years, but now he was to be daily committed to the requests of his ordinary, Bishop Quinn, and of the priests and faithful of this huge diocese.

Person to Person, Family to Family

As a bishop of Hispanic background, the new auxiliary shared a paramount concern for a minority population united linguistically by the common usage of the Spanish language and a common religious heritage but widely diverse in terms of integration into American society. There were those who had historical ties with long-term, even pre–North American, presence in the great Southwest of the United States.[2] There were also those who by education had entered into the cultural context of the American middle class. The significant feature, however, of migratory patterns in the second half of the twentieth century was the massive movement of Spanish-speaking laborers, farmworkers, and youth from various Latin American countries to the north in search of improving their standard of living and helping the families left behind in their native countries. Their poverty and lack of civil status left them vulnerable to exploitation. Concern for the migrant had surfaced in various pastoral appeals on the part of the American hierarchy and in the very elevation of Hispanic clerics to share in the outreach to the migrant population. The new bishops gave voice to the overriding need for a program of pastoral care and evangelization adapted to the Hispanics.

An excellent example of this pastoral awareness is to be found in the *Letter of the Hispanic Bishops of California to the Hispanic People of California,* coauthored by six Hispanic bishops of the Golden State, including Bishop Gallegos of Sacramento.[3] It was intended to complement several previous documents issued by the United States Catholic Conference relative to the phenomenon of the Hispanic migration to and presence in the United States.[4] The title of the document bespeaks a pastoral approach that would be closely aligned to the evangelical style already employed by Bishop Gallegos during his years of church leadership in Sacramento.

The California bishops reiterated the core message of the American hierarchy's analysis of the "Hispanic presence" as a blessing for the church and the nation, a time of grace not to be lost by acts of discrimination or prejudice. In the body of the text of "The Joy of Being Catholic," the bishops sought to bring the message of hope and concern to their local constituencies by referring directly to the fears and unsettled social and legal situations of the migrant. With very incisive language, they also reminded their Hispanic brothers and sisters of the dangers of losing their religious convictions and cultural identity due to the inroads of proselytizing non-Catholic sects among the newly arrived immigrants. They clarified for their readers the difference between true ecumenism, a necessary feature of a pluralistic society such as the United States, and a kind of aggressive fundamentalism looking to benefit from the cultural displacement in which the migrant frequently found himself.

The document, written in the later years of Bishop Gallegos's pastoral activities in Sacramento, reflects by retrospection the priorities that had governed his actions as bishop. He would counter the claims of the fundamentalists as divisive and disrespectful of family and cultural bonds and encourage fidelity to the inherited customs of a Catholic religious culture rich in celebration and the skills of family and community living. The reasons for "joy" as described in the "Joy of Being Catholic" are the sacraments and sacramental life of the church, the traditions of faith and worship and, in a special way, devotion to Mary, Mother of Jesus, particularly, under the title of Our Lady of Guadalupe.

A Ministry of Joy

As of the date of his episcopal ordination, Bishop Gallegos was named vicar general of the Diocese of Sacramento. Early in 1982, he informed the provincial of the Augustinian Recollects that a successor had been named to the post of director of Hispanic affairs for the California Catholic Conference and that he had moved to his new office at the chancery at 1119 K Street. In the same letter, he enthusiastically comments that he could now dedicate himself "to the needs of the Diocese of Sacramento," which, for the bishop, began with the "circuit of Confirmation, which I find exciting for it gives me an opportunity to meet the faithful of the diocese, priests and religious."[5]

Although the condition of his eyesight continued to deteriorate to the extent that

> he was unable to see or read documents unless they were typed in very large fonts...for all practical purposes, he ignored or tried to ignore his eye infirmity, and in the seven years that I served as his personal secretary, he never mentioned or referred to it.[6]

Although he formed part of the administrative team of the diocese, his clear preference was for direct pastoral involvement with the people of the diocese.

> His pastoral approach was a person-to-person one. He showed special concern for the youth and their education, and established scholarships and gave monetary assistance to needy students. He was always available for visits to the elderly and the sick and showed special concern for them, as well as for all minority groups. However, he never excluded anybody.[7]

Upon being named pastor of the Church of Our Lady of Guadalupe in the city of Sacramento on June 27, 1983, he found a center for serving the largely Mexican community of the capital city and environs. The church had been dedicated to Our Lady of Guadalupe on April 16, 1945, and, after the construction of a new facility to replace the old, it was made a "national" parish for the Spanish-speaking in 1969 by Bishop Alden Bell, Sacramento ordinary at the time.[8] It had become the largest parish in the diocese, with a Mass attendance of nearly three thousand at the Sunday liturgies. An interesting "Report of the Problem of the Church and the Spanish-Speaking People in the Diocese of Sacramento (February 1963)" was undoubtedly available to the new pastor as he attempted to take up the role of shepherding a large congregation in conditions of constant growth. The 1963 report, prepared by "a number of priests of the Diocese of Sacramento, concerning or working with the Spanish-Speaking people of this diocese" under the leadership of Father Keith Kenny, administrator of Our Lady of Guadalupe at the time, enumerates a series of obstacles to the evangelization of the Hispanics of the diocese.[9] A key problem noted by the authors was and remained that of the encounter between an established church community and a new population of non-English-speaking immigrants, resulting in cultural and linguistic differences. At the core of the problem, as commented in the report, was the lack of Spanish-speaking clergy to attend to the needs of the Hispanic population. Language, of course, is more than language; it embraces a cultural attitude and expressions that color the habitual modes of social and religious life among the various linguistic groups.

A similar document (March 11, 1965), forwarded to Bishop Bell and authored by Father Kenny, summarizes the plight of the approximately thirty-five thousand Mexicans living in the Sacramento metropolitan area as "culturally deprived, economically deprived, religiously deprived."[10] Among the insightful recommendations to be found in the pastoral proposal was the strong emphasis given to an evangelizing strategy that would center on the family. The family is identified in the conclusions of this document as "the most cogent factor, most important relationship, and the only society in which they [the Mexicans] feel security."[11]

It would not be surprising that the new pastor of Our Lady of Guadalupe would carry into practice a program of home visitation. Bringing the faith to the homes of local families had been a practice that he had initiated even in the early years of his priesthood. Gerald and Reseanne Lalumiere remember fondly the visits of the young, nearsighted Father Gallegos, who, after Sunday Mass at Holy Rosary Church in Greenwood Lake, New York, not far from Tagaste Monastery, "would just come and join our family for dinner and our eight children would love the way he would just settle in their midst as if he were one of them."[12] His frequent and spontaneous visits to families had been commonplace during his years at San Miguel. One of his volunteer drivers for that period attests that "he had a great charisma of being 'present' to people, and would not exclude anyone from an encounter with him merely on past history, appearance, reputation or social standing."[13] Patricia Villavazo of La Palma, California, had witnessed this never-excluding care practiced by the pastor of San Miguel when, on a Sunday afternoon, she had seen Father Gallegos lifting an intoxicated man from the street and carrying him to the rectory, where he cared for the unfortunate man until he was ready to leave on his own.[14] Such testimonies concerning the future auxiliary bishop of Sacramento are legion and are not confined simply to his years at San Miguel and Cristo Rey.

As bishop, Gallegos had time for everyone, and his desk agenda was filled with little notations indicating home visits, birthdays, and, frequently, home celebrations of the Eucharist. His style would soon catch the attention of the Sacramento press. One journalist summed it up in the headline: "Hispanic bishop doesn't wait for followers to come to him."[15] He had made the news because he had launched a campaign to help the immigrants apply for legal status made possible by a liberalization of the immigration restrictions for nonlegal residents, and, at the same time, he was raising funds for a little girl in Peru in need of a liver transplant. The journalist wrote that, although "Gallegos has a desk in the Chancery...he is rarely behind it." He was referring to the fact that, beyond the parish of Our Lady of Guadalupe, Bishop Gallegos traveled extensively through the 43,000-square-mile diocese, especially to reach the camps and scattered barrios of the migrant workers. In reply to the journalist, Father Al, as he liked to be called, stated that "I make it a point to be on the ranches and farms...to make the people feel, by our presence, that we are one church."[16] It was, he told the newspaperman, something that he had seen as a youngster among the parish priests at San Miguel, that is, "developing a one-to-one relationship to the people."[17]

The person-to-person, family-to-family style of evangelization did not, however, exclude a public, more political role; indeed, he had been named to one of the commissions of California's Advisory Council by Governor George Deukmejian in 1984. He saw himself nonetheless more as a "dispenser of Word and Sacrament" in the tradition of Saint Augustine. Such was the tactic that he employed relative to two high-priority groups: the young and the migrant. A typical example of his style of evangelizing youth is contained in an account of his return to Cristo Rey in 1990 to conduct a parish mission and a retreat for the young.

> Bishop Gallegos arrived in the late afternoon to conduct a Mission Series. Each day he was available for private talks, confessions and home and hospital visits. He walked the streets and talked with as many of the youth as he could, inviting them to the Mission and to return to the community of Christ. He dedicated Thursday, Oct. 11, to all the youth, celebrating the Mass bilingually but predominantly in English, with a strong talk on the importance of family communication, respect for self, peers and parents, and imitating Christ. Thursday evening Bishop Gallegos was hearing confessions into midnight.[18]

The Youth Are the "Church of Today Even If They Are Not Going to Church"

In December 1990, *Revista Maryknoll* published the second of two articles on the Hispanic auxiliary bishop of Sacramento. The first, entitled "Bishop for the Youth" and published at an earlier date, in March 1982, praised the prelate of the "low-rider culture" for his approach to the youth, which were described by Gallegos as "the Church of today even if they are not going to Church."[19] Such openness to the "unchurched" arose from his acceptance of a pastoral responsibility to reach out to the alienated rather than assume a posture of distancing himself from the religiously and socially marginal groups. He simply responded to the well-known journalist of Hispanic news, Moisés Sandoval, that "we have to show them [the youth] they are part of the Church."[20]

The later article, "Cerca de los Campesinos," by the same writer, explores the scope of Gallegos's involvement with the widely dispersed migrant labor population of the diocese. The reporter refers to the twenty-five worker camps located throughout the extensive San Joaquín Valley, famous as one of the main sources of food production for the American consumers as well as for exportation to the nations of the Pacific Rim. Bishop Gallegos once made the comment to another reporter that

> we in the United States can better appreciate the work of the undocumented, which is mainly agricultural by thanking God for the food we have on our table—the fruits and vegetables—because we ourselves do not want to get into that kind of laborious work.[21]

This production depended upon the *bracero* or migrant worker who would come to the fields at harvest or planting seasons from the various states of Mexico or the southern border states of the United States. Some would arrive with wife and children; the majority, however, would have left their families behind in their hometowns.

As frequently as possible, Bishop Alphonse visited the camps with a team of religious sisters and lay volunteers who would assist in preparing the children for the sacraments. Indeed, he was credited by Cardinal Roger Mahony, archbishop of Los Angeles, for having been the spark that set in motion the mobile pastoral teams for farm workers throughout California, as well as the Spanish language radio programs that reached migrant farm workers in California and in Mexico.[22]

The bishop forfeited vacations in order to make time to remain, if possible, for a week's duration to know better the spiritual and material conditions of the men and women in these camps. At times alone, or accompanied by his auxiliary, Bishop Quinn would also celebrate the Eucharist in these camps. Due to the absence of churches or chapels, the Mass was usually celebrated in an outside patio with song and joyful participation. Bishop Al, as was customary with him, would invite the children to gather around the altar. His simple message was to remind the congregation that, although lacking the physical structure of a church building, they, with their bishop, were indeed "church."

Gallegos summarized his position on the undocumented and the migrant in an official statement that was issued for publication.

> We strongly support assistance for those who come to the United States seeking asylum from countries suffering political repression and economic hardship. The newcomers should be welcome and not manipulated for political or self-serving reasons. The Church must respond by offering these people safety, food, clothing, health care and spiritual assistance. Our concern is not to support any particular effort that assists the refugees or immigrants, but to help them in the tradition of Christian ministry. And we should minister to their physical and spiritual needs without regard to their country of origin or their political beliefs. In doing this, we should be Christ-like and exclude no one.[23]

His emphasis on the sacraments and on devotion, especially to Our Lady of Guadalupe, in no way meant that he was unaware of or indifferent to the precarious and unhealthy conditions in which the migrant often lived and worked. Bishop Gallegos had marched with Cesar Chavez, the courageous leader of the United Farm Workers, and remained close to him as both struggled to obtain more just conditions for the workers and better treatment for the undocumented. As Congressman Robert T. Matsui commented in the *Congressional Record,*

> Bishop Gallegos was a forceful advocate for the concerns of the Hispanics. He marched in solidarity with the United Farm Workers, opposed cuts in bilingual education, and worked with inner-city gangs up and down the State. He worked tirelessly to steer Hispanic youth toward education and away from drugs and crime.[24]

He used his office as vicar for ethnic minorities to address not only the plight of the Hispanic but also to stand by the African Americans, the Native Americans, the Koreans, and other ethnic groups seeking a voice and recognition within the church of Sacramento. He enjoyed celebrating multiple birthday parties with the different ethnic groups. Not to be forgotten on his agenda were the prisoners at Folsom Prison, who received his visits twice a year. He would spend an entire day with them, from 9:00 a.m. to 10:00 p.m., giving them a "mission."

Especially for the Unborn and the Unwanted

Reporting on the tragic death of Bishop Alphonse, which occurred on Sunday afternoon, October 6, 1991, Michael Wood wrote in the Sacramento diocesan newspaper that, on that same afternoon,

> Bishop Gallegos, who was strongly dedicated to the pro-life cause, participated in the Capital Life Chain, a peaceful demonstration against abortion in which people lined up for one hour along Sunrise Boulevard and Greenback Lane in the Citrus Heights area, each holding signs saying "Abortion Kills Children" or, a sign like Bishop Gallegos held, "Jesus Forgives and Heals."[25]

The sign held by the bishop appropriately expresses his attitude toward the pro-abortion demonstrators on the other side of the street. He had told the story of crossing the street on another occasion of opposing demonstrations in order to show that he was also praying for the conversion of the misguided supporters of abortion.[26] On that same day of his death, he had visited and consoled a young male patient dying of AIDS.[27]

His appreciation for the gift of life extended from the unborn to the chronically sick and to the mentally handicapped. Maria Navarro, who will later play an important role in the construction of the statue in honor of the deceased bishop, recalls a tender moment in the life of her family that well describes the sensitivity of her pastor.

> I had a sister who was moderately retarded. She and Bishop Gallegos both celebrated their birthdays on the 20th of February. Once, when the community of Santa Ana Church honored Bishop Gallegos' birthday, he asked me to sing Ave Maria after dinner. I gladly agreed to sing and, when he thanked me afterwards, I told him that my sister Chavela also celebrated her birthday on the 20th of February. Without further ado, he picked up the small vase of flowers that was in front of him at the table and took it to Chavela at our table. When he presented her with the flowers, he sang a Spanish birthday song, "Las Mañanitas," to her.[28]

Consistent with his chain of life ethic, Bishop Gallegos, as reported in the *New York Times,* had been among the protesters attempting to block the shipment of atomic warheads to the Trident submarine bases on the west coast.[29] He perceived clearly the deadly logic that links the practice of abortion to the other techniques of destruction proper to the "culture of death." There were innumerable occasions, in a politically charged state capital such as Sacramento, for the bishop to be called upon to give the invocation or blessing at a civic event or gathering. Inevitably, he would include a plea for the unborn in his prayer. It was not at all surprising, therefore, that shortly after his death a Bishop Gallegos Maternity Home was opened for the benefit of unwed mothers. Bishop Francis Quinn recognized the close association between the dedication of the recently deceased auxiliary and the purpose of the home. "It is appropriate," he said, "that this maternity home be dedicated to the memory of Bishop Gallegos, because of his persistent and untiring efforts on behalf of the unborn."[30] That same month of December, the supporters of life organized a Holy Innocents candlelight procession in his honor.[31]

Diocesan Pastoral Plan for the Hispanic Ministry/*Plan Pastoral Diocesano para el Ministerio Hispano*

Often what is sown gestates slowly before it comes to fruition. The earlier "Report of the Problem of the Church and the Spanish-Speaking People in the Diocese of Sacramento" and the "Pastoral Proposal I" conscientiously addressed the socio-cultural situation of the Spanish-speaking on the basis of the findings of the eminent Belgian priest and sociologist, Canon Houtart of the University of Louvain. He had concluded, with reference to the assimilation of the immigrant into the

American Catholic Church, that there was a relationship between the availability of "native speaking clergy" and programs and the immigrant's fidelity to his traditional religion.[32] Where such culture-friendly parish environments did not exist, the foreign newcomer could easily be lost to the proselytizing fundamentalist sects. The six Hispanic bishops of California squarely faced this phenomenon of the loss of religious faith and adherence to the Catholic traditions in their collective letter of 1988, *The Joy of Being Catholic/El Gozo de ser Católico.* The need to respond to the challenge of the Hispanic presence was becoming more urgent with each passing generation.

The statistics recorded in the earlier report and pastoral proposal had changed greatly by the time Bishop Alphonse became vicar episcopal for the Hispanics and Other Ethnic Ministries. By 1990, there were 22.4 million Hispanics in the United States, and, in the Diocese of Sacramento, Hispanics constituted close to 50 percent of the Catholic population, compared with something more than 25 percent on the basis of the 1960 census. The Hispanics had also acquired a greater voice in the political and social arena as a result not only of numbers but also as a result of the Chicano movement of the 1960s.

One of the institutions that benefited from the assignment of Bishop Gallegos to Our Lady of Guadalupe Church as pastor was the expansion of the Centro Guadalupe, a building across the alley from the church that hosted a service center attending to the material and spiritual needs of the mostly Mexican and Mexican American populations of metropolitan Sacramento. It also sponsored a variety of programs of formation and information to its clients. As a direct result of the pastor's efforts and the support of the parishioners and others, Holy Angels' School, close to the parish and closed down since 1972, was transformed, in the mid-1980s, into the Hispanic Institute for Learning. These parochial experiences, plus the pastoral outreach to the migrant workers, were based on the bishop's firm conviction that a pastor's relationship to the people he serves is one of reciprocity in grace, mutually enriching to both in shared wisdom and faith.

Extrapolating from the particular experience of parish life and always with the paradigm of Watts alive in his memory, Bishop Al initiated the elaboration of a *Diocesan Pastoral Plan for Hispanic Ministry/Plan Pastoral Diocesano para el Ministerio Hispano*. After two years of intense collaboration among a variety of representatives, clergy, religious, and the laity, the plan was published in a bilingual edition in April 1991—just six months prior to the bishop's death—by the Diocese of Sacramento.

From the first page to the last of the fourteen-page document, it is evident that the work was a cooperative effort in which many voices were heard and many ideas were brought into focus in the process of prayerful dialogue. The tone is set in the preface.

> Since Vatican II, we have been invited to share in communion and co-responsibility. All members of God's people must work in communion; evangelization would not be credible nor appropriate if it appears to be an action of an individual and not a mission which the whole Christian Community must fulfill.[33]

The objective of the plan is revealed in the concept, "From Vision to Realization," which "Vision" is spelled out in four specific dimensions or general objectives: (1) Pastoral de Conjunto—from fragmentation to coordination; (2) Evangelization—from a place to a home; (3) Missionary—from pews to shoes; (4) Formation—from good will to skills.[34] Each of these dimensions is subject to further elaboration in the text that follows. No doubt the document highlights some of the principal values accentuated in Bishop Gallegos's understanding of church and pastoral theology. The leadership of the ordinary, Bishop Quinn, and his auxiliary is affirmed, and the theology of a collaborative ministry is elicited from the document of the Bishops of the United States published in December 1983 under the title, *The Hispanic Presence: Challenge and Commitment*. Ideological support for creating a planned pastoral approach to the Hispanic is also to be found in the declarations of the 1985 Third National Hispanic *Encuentro*.[35]

Throughout the text, two guiding themes animated the working groups that were drawing up priorities and goals for each of the general objectives. These were a love for Holy Mother Church and a "loving recognition of those who have preceded us in preserving the Catholic faith in the Diocese of Sacramento."[36] No two themes could be more familiar to or appreciated by Bishop Gallegos than these. He could not help but recall the household of faith and Catholic tradition in which he had been raised. Bishop Quinn commended Bishop Gallegos and "all his co-workers who have prepared this first diocesan Hispanic Congress, and beseech God's grace on our Hispanic Pastoral Plan."[37] A special page had been intercalated in the text of the plan preceding Bishop Quinn's letter. It was a page entitled "In Memoriam 1931–1991" above a photograph of Most Rev. Alphonse Gallegos, auxiliary bishop of Sacramento. Death came to the energetic Hispanic bishop in a tragic way on October 6, 1991. Perhaps, the plan was a kind of last testament.

Gentle Man, Loving Priest, Caring Bishop

It Happened on the Feast of the Holy Rosary

He had never seen a funeral quite like it, was the comment of Monsignor Edward Kavanagh, a veteran pastor of more than fifty years in the city of Sacramento, when asked about the final tribute paid to Bishop Alphonse Gallegos. It had been at St. Rose Parish that Father Al, under the guidance of Monsignor Kavanagh, began his pastoral activity in Sacramento. The bishop had been buried in the bishops' crypt in St. Mary's Cemetery following the Mass of Christian Burial celebrated in the presence of more than two thousand faithful at Blessed Sacrament Cathedral on Friday, October 11, 1991.

News had reached the city swiftly on Sunday evening, October 6, that the Hispanic auxiliary bishop had met instant death in an automobile accident along the darkened corridors of Highway 99 near Yuba City. The story of the tragic episode quickly reached a stunned capital city. Santiago Ruiz, one of the volunteer drivers who drove for the bishop and the solitary witness of what had happened, was interviewed by the police and representatives of the media.[1] The details of what had occurred captivated the public's attention during the week that followed.

Sunday, October 6, 1991, was the start of a typically busy day for the bishop. In addition to the liturgy at Our Lady of Guadalupe, there was a list of pastoral visits to be made on the way to Gridley, a town 75 miles north of Sacramento, and to the parish of the Sacred Heart, where he was to confirm seventy Hispanic youngsters. The list, more in the mind than on paper, was a sample of his multiple concerns for others. On the way to Gridley, he was there in the Capital Life Chain to pray and lend support to the pro-life advocates. And, then, there was the young man dying of AIDS whom he wished to visit. On the lighter side, they had to drop by the parish of St. Joseph to share a festive moment with the parishioners. Before getting on the highway to Gridley, the bishop found time to accompany a group of Korean Catholics who were scouting properties in search of a site for a future church.

Finally, he arrived at Gridley. After celebrating the Liturgy of Confirmation and sharing in the reception that followed, Bishop Al and his driver left to return to Sacramento, in spite of the Gridley pastor's plea that they stay overnight due to the lateness of the hour. But, with a pressing Monday schedule on the horizon, the bishop decided to go home. Santiago Ruiz was driving along Highway 99, so often traveled before by the bishop on the way to the migrant camps, heading south in the bishop's 1984 Volkswagen Jetta. He had had trouble with the electrical system of the old car, but he was not one to spend money on anything but a used car.

They were reciting the rosary, according to the testimony of the driver, when the car stalled in the fast lane of the highway. The bishop got out of the car, in spite of the protests of the driver, in order to lend a hand to pushing the car to the side of the road. He was on the passenger side of the vehicle. In an instant, another car traveling in the same direction struck the stalled vehicle and the bishop from behind, propelling the bishop's body 50 to 60 feet into the bushes on the right shoulder of the highway. Ruiz was thrown against the highway divider and suffered minor injuries. An investigation of the accident cleared the driver of the impacting vehicle of any charges. The accident occurred at 9:18 p.m.[2]

A stunned city awoke to the somber news on Monday morning, the feast of the Holy Rosary. Bishop Quinn spoke for all as he described the death of his episcopal colleague as a "sad hour" for the diocese and the church of California. The preparations were underway for a time of mourning and for the final Christian farewell to a man who had been a source of so much joy and enthusiasm among the people of Sacramento. On the morning of October 10, prior to the celebration of the 8:00 a.m. Eucharist, the body of Bishop Gallegos was escorted into his beloved Church of Our Lady of Guadalupe. An all-day vigil was held. "One by one, they arrived at Our Lady of Guadalupe Church in Sacramento. They included the Black Catholic Council, a group of Vietnamese refugees, contingents of Filipinos, Hispanic and Polish-Americans."[3] In the evening the body was transferred to the Blessed Sacrament Cathedral, where vigil service was held. The prior provincial of the Augustinian Recollects, representing the religious order in which Bishop Gallegos had made his first vows as a religious, brought to light the spirituality of the young friar Gallegos so aptly defined by Alphonse as the offering of "a grain of incense," a sacrifice of self to the will of God.[4]

More than two dozen bishops and more than one hundred priests in addition to scores of religious sisters and brothers filed into Blessed Sacrament Cathedral as part of the tide of more than two thousand mourners that filled the church, with the overflow occupying the plaza in front of the mother church of the Diocese of Sacramento. Bishop Francis Quinn presided at the Liturgy of Christian Burial, so rich in the theme of the resurrection, and His

Eminence, Roger Cardinal Mahony of the Archdiocese of Los Angeles, preached an insightful and fraternal homily that brilliantly captured the spiritual and pastoral charism of the man whose earthly remains, vested in the symbols of his office, reposed in front of the altar, the source of his great-hearted priesthood.

Underscoring the spiritual principles that were fundamental for Bishop Alphonse, Cardinal Mahony mentioned that

> first...one needs a strong spiritual life in order to know Jesus deeply and personally: otherwise how are we to recognize him in others. And second, that frequent pastoral visits are essential to bringing food and drink to those in need, to discover the stranger and the ill, to bring comfort to the imprisoned and abandoned.[5]

These qualities of a deep interior life and pastoral zeal were so evident in the life of Bishop Gallegos that Cardinal Mahony, in perfect consonance with the congregation present, could rightly concluded his homily by honoring the deceased as "a gentle man, a loving priest, a caring bishop."[6] In a similar vein, Bishop Quinn, in a public tribute to his brother bishop, summed up the general feeling: "Bishop Gallegos was characterized by a love for the Church, a joyful, optimistic spirit and a courageous ability to overcome adversity."[7] Little wonder that the mayor of Sacramento, Anne Rudin, was led to remark, "I have never seen such a diverse group come to pay tribute to any one person in Sacramento."[8]

The worshiping union formed among these diverse groups joined the caravan to St. Mary's Cemetery. The Sacramento Custom Car and Truck Association organized a procession to accompany the bishop's body, first, from Our Lady of Guadalupe to the cathedral, and then from the cathedral to the cemetery. It could not have been anything less for one who had been for them the "low-rider bishop." After all, they had been with him with cars and lanterns on the day of his consecration as bishop. Native Americans in traditional dress, the Knights of St. Peter Claver, an African American society of which he was a member, the Asian communities, and the multitude of his Hispanic and non-Hispanic friends prayed at the tomb and, then, left for home. They felt diminished by the loss but, at the same time, elevated and graced by knowing that a man of the church of such unusual sanctity and spiritual greatness of heart had been among them and had touched their lives. Among those close to the crypt were the bishop's brothers and sisters with their by-now adult children. The heaviness that gripped their hearts at the moment was lightened by the intimate remembrances of a loving brother who had achieved so much good since those days of playing priest in the house of José and Caciana.

CHAPTER 8

Burnt Tortillas and a Statue

Death is closure, a kind of finality that tends to sweep into the vortex of the past even the most pristine of remembrances. There are, however, recollections still vibrant in the memories of those who had been inspired by the remembered works of those whose goodness somehow transcends the clouds of forgetfulness. It is in remembering that humankind pastes together the fragments of the past into a kind of mosaic for the present.

In the case of Bishop Gallegos, according to one young journalist in Sacramento, there were rumors in the barrio. Writing in 1995, the same journalist said, "Even today, people are agonizing over how best to preserve his memory."[1] Bob Sylva, the newspaperman, was listening to the conversations in the barrio. The great photographs that had appeared in the newspapers during the week of mourning had often caught the celebratory and playful charm of the barrio's particular prelate. There was the white cowboy hat worn at parish fiestas, the beaming smile, the embrace of children, but, perhaps, something was needed to brighten the memories of the folks in Sacramento's Hispanic neighborhoods. Sylva discovered an amateur playwright who wanted to do something to remind the people of the joy and lightheartedness that radiated from the bishop whom he had first known as "Father Al" during those Friday night tours along Franklin Boulevard. Richard Alcala, known as "Flaco," had never written a thing in his thirty-seven years of life. As an ordinary worker at the Campbell Soup factory, he was not exactly called upon to do creative writing. What gnawed at him, however, was the fear that the chaplain of the "low-riders" would be forgotten.

Richard had an idea for a story and a play that would show the local audience at the St. Rose Church social hall just what kind of man was this bishop who, perhaps, was beginning to fade from their memories. He chose a really intriguing title that, while not easily understood by someone outside of the barrio, would certainly bring smiles to the Mexican faces in the audience. Burnt tortillas are like burnt toast, not exactly the best fare to offer for a meal. The story went around, however, that, when Alfonso was a kid at home, his sisters would, by distraction, forgetfulness, or playfulness, burn the tortillas. It apparently happened so often that Alfonso, instead of getting angry or hostile, would say, "But I like burnt tortillas." Somebody must have revealed this family secret, maybe Al himself. It had been, for him, an example of simple patience that he used humorously to invite his listeners in church or on retreat to consider. By accepting with generosity and good humor the little crosses of life, the bigger crosses, when they come along, will not be so heavy.

The result of Richard Alcala's first attempt at writing was *Burnt Tortillas: The Bishop Gallegos Story.* Beginning with the theme of generous acceptance, the author traces the self-sacrificing goodwill exuded by Bishop Al in his ministry to others, leading up to the act of love that marked the hours of his last day on Earth, Sunday, October 6, 1991. It was a kind of morality play for the barrio. And, as to the beneficiary of the evenings' entertainment, all proceeds would go to the Bishop Gallegos Scholarship Fund. His constant appeal for an educated youth had not fallen on deaf ears. The budding playwright confesses that he created this memorial because

> I think the community needs to believe in somebody. He believed that everyone should work together, to help

each other. That no one is better than anyone else. He was very friendly, very humble. A simple message. He never asked anything for himself.[2]

The greatest legacy left by the bishop, in the opinion of the editors of the *Catholic Herald,* was his "devotion to Mary," which "must be treasured, fostered and constantly renewed."[3] Devotion to Mary was a common denominator among the cultures that Bishop Alphonse sought to serve in his apostolate. No doubt, his deep attachment to the rosary, inherited from family prayer and enhanced by his poverty of vision, had given him access to the mysteries of faith in a pure and simple way, unencumbered by the weight of theological treatises. He was forced by circumstances to operate in an oral culture rather than in a reading culture. The rosary summarized his personal Bible. In a sermon dedicated to "Mary, Mother of the Poor," Bishop Alphonse perceives the mission of Mary in the church as one of hope and healing, an enduring example of God's love for the human family.[4]

The idea of erecting a monument of remembrance that would occupy a physical space in the city of Sacramento was gaining acceptance and enthusiastic support. A "Rose Garden for Peace," with a dedicatory plaque in honor of the bishop, was set in place on the grounds of Our Lady of Guadalupe Church. It was designed by T. J. David, president of International World Peace Rose Gardens. But something else was stirring in the community, and, after conversations and hesitations, a committee was formed to realize an ambitious project, which would be to erect a sculpted image of Bishop Alphonse Gallegos in bronze to be placed between the Cathedral and the state Capitol. It was no simple task to arrive at the consensus that resulted in the election of María Navarro as chairwoman of the project and the selection of her husband, George, as treasurer. Both María and George had been active in civic affairs in the city of Sacramento, often in the forefront of causes on behalf of their Hispanic neighbors. They developed their plans and strategies with the assistance of ten additional committee members, including the mayor of Sacramento, Joe Serna, Jr.

Some questioned the wisdom of the project, for fear that it could be politicized as a type of confrontational symbol in the constant strivings of the minorities for social justice and equal rights. Others were critical because they questioned the inclusion among the supporters of the project of some public figures who had not been politically comfortable with the bishop's strong pro-life position. The idea of the committee, however, was to remind the people of Sacramento of the late bishop's all-embracing practice of his Augustinian motto, "Love one another." There were sensitive moments, but the project went forward.

Robert Houser, a sculptor from El Paso, Texas, was chosen to create a 7-foot bronze image of Bishop Gallegos that was to be elevated on a pedestal and located on 11th Street between the Cathedral and the state Capitol building. The pedestrian corridor along 11th Street that leads to the Capitol was renamed "Bishop Gallegos Square." The committee raised the needed $38,000 among a wide diversity of citizens and institutions of the capital city. The sculptor expressed his sentiments in a statement provided for the dedication booklet.

> I have sought to commit to Bronze the memory of a man as he still lives within the hearts of his friends and associates. In doing so, I had the pleasure of rediscovering those qualities that made him loved among you. Embodied in sculpture, this symbol of the man and his ideals will confront generations. Should this work then stir those echoes of his personality in history and inspire a rededication to his motto: "Love One Another," it will endure both as a celebration of his purpose and as a confirmation of my efforts.[5]

On February 23, 1997, three years after the initiation of the project and on a date close to what would have been Alfonso's sixty-seventh birthday, February 20, the "low-riders" lifted the veil covering the statue to the applause and admiration of those present. Close to the statue were the sisters, brothers, nieces, and nephews of the bishop. They had always been there for him and he for them. The children and grandchildren of José and Caciana were living a moment of heaven-sent pride and gratitude.

A bilingual liturgy had preceded the unveiling, bringing together priests and laity of the diocese with Bishop William Weigand, new ordinary of the Sacramento Diocese, presiding as principal celebrant. Bishop Francis Quinn, now retired as ordinary, preached the homily. At the unveiling ceremony, Bishop Quinn once again recognized those qualities in his auxiliary that had endeared him to the people of the diocese and elsewhere. Notable among those characteristics was his unfailing love of the church, his joy and optimism. Not to be forgotten was Bishop Alphonse's courage in the face of adversity; the eyeglasses on the sculpted figure would remind those who knew him of his lifelong struggle with the shadows of seriously deformed eyesight. At the same time, Sacramento's new prelate, Bishop Weigand, saw the image and the locale of its emplacement as a reminder of the deceased bishop's role as a "bridge" between the teachings of Jesus and the lawmakers at the state Capitol down the street. The music provided by the Mariachi Zacatecas created a festive atmosphere, while the old friends of the bishop, the "low-riders" and dancing Native Americans, surrounded his family with the affection of a city that would be forever graced by his likeness along the graceful corridor now bearing his name, Bishop Gallegos Square.[6]

CHAPTER 9

Lessons in Spirituality

To describe the spirituality of Bishop Alphonse Gallegos, OAR, on the basis of a study of documents might lead the investigator to a seemingly small number of such written materials. There is no evidence of what might be called an extensive "paper trail." It is necessary to keep in mind the bishop's reliance upon auditory rather than visual modes of communication. As has been noted, he lived and functioned within an oral culture. Although he made some use of the typewriter, not yet into the computer age, he spoke and preached most frequently without notes or only with a few large lettered outlines on the paper. These written documents, most often unsigned, are recognizably his on the basis of the large font employed. A more extensive source for his public is to be found in tape recordings and videos.

The choice of the phrase, "Love one another," was far from haphazard. It was for him the primordial imperative of the gospel, thus, Christ's command to love was considered the unifying theme of Christ's mission and the essential reason for his incarnate presence. The fact that the future auxiliary bishop of Sacramento chose this saying as his pastoral motto, to be emblazoned on his coat of arms, reveals both a certain humble simplicity of his own understanding of his calling and an attachment to one of the permanent sources of his spirituality, which was the monastic *Rule of St. Augustine.* The Augustinian component of his spiritual and religious formation synchronized perfectly with the Christian formation that he had received in a family united in faith and the Catholic tradition.

The Gallegos family, formed and nurtured lovingly by José Gallegos and Caciana Apodaca, received from the traditions of their ancestors in New Mexico, with its Spanish religiosity, a profound love for the church and for the devotions that gave meaning to the daily lives of parents and children. The family itself assumed the initial task of catechizing, creating thereby an environment of joyful religiosity. Both as pastor of California parishes and as bishop, Alphonse would draw abundantly from his experience as one of eleven children in a working-class migrant family as he repeatedly returned to the theme of the family as core value of the Hispanic tradition and an essential basis for Christian living. In a charming conference given in Spanish and entitled "Los Abuelos en el Seno de la Familia," he takes to task those Hispanics who had forgotten their traditional care for the elderly and reminds them of the continuity of life and caring for life from generation to generation. What the young Alphonse learned from the family in the art of loving helped him to fashion his consistent habit of home visitations and in sharing the table of the poor.

The formation, which Alphonse enjoyed at home with his brothers and sisters, was not closed off from the world but rather led to their active involvement in joining the neighbors in developing the new parish of San Miguel. "Love one another" was practiced in the barrio with Marian devotions and, of course, the Saint Joseph vigil at the Gallegos's home, to which the neighbors were invited. The Gallegos family, with the other families of Watts, made the parish their home, where they took an active role and where Alphonse found a community of religious interested in encouraging a near-blind altar boy to think about a religious vocation. This friendly openness introduced the young Alphonse to a new possibility of learning how to put in practice the gospel injunction to "love one another" according to an ancient source of Christian spirituality, namely, the *Rule of St. Augustine* as lived by the Augustinian Recollect friars at San Miguel Parish. Later, as a novice at the Augustinian Recollect house of formation in Kansas City, Kansas, he studied the *Rule* and listened to the Friday reading of the same in Latin during the meals served in silence at the refectory. He could not help but be impressed by the solemn invitation with which Saint Augustine begins his *Rule.* "Before all else, beloved brothers, let us love God and then our neighbor, because these are the principal commandments given to us."[1] The precepts of the *Rule* are the requirements for fulfilling the "main purpose for which you have come together [which] is to live harmoniously in the house and to have one soul and one heart intent upon God."[2]

The extent of the influence of his formation as an Augustinian Recollect is clearly exposed in a conference that he gave to the religious of Sacramento under the title of "Religious in the Twentieth Century."[3] His teaching on the vows, following in the spirit of Vatican II, demonstrates a firm grasp of the topic as well as the experience of a former novice master and prefect of professed religious. In the conference, he is critical of what he sees to be an inadequate response to renewal in the wake of Vatican II. He called out for a more authentic living of religious poverty. He asks, "Has this vow meant for us a mere poverty of permission to live like the average American? Has it made us comfortably secure?"[4] In his own ascent to the episcopacy, Alphonse continued to think of himself as a religious and personally, while not canonically, bound to observe poverty. When asked on an official form about a last will and testament, he stated simply that it was on file with the Augustinian Recollects, referring to the profession of poverty that he made upon occasion of embracing his solemn vows in 1954.[5] He used whatever income he received chiefly to pay the tuition for needy students at the Catholic schools in the area. A witness to the fact affirms that, upon examining the bedroom of the bishop after his death, she found a room as austere and sparse as a monk's cell.[6]

In the same document, the bishop exhorts his audience of religious to embrace chastity as a faith-inspired way to attain "better community living,"[7] which means relating to one another in "warmth and friendship."[8] Certainly, such a notion of a community resonating the values of fraternity would be a reflection of his own appreciation for the *Rule of St. Augustine*. While respecting the requirements of the law in the practice of obedience, he sees, in a legalistic concept of obedience, a flawed understanding of that which should be an obedience viewed as a "loving response to God in imitation of and in company with Christ."[9] Without doubt, the bishop considered religious life to be an apostolic way of life rooted, however, in an exemplary community life. During his ten years as auxiliary bishop of Sacramento, he maintained an affectionate bond with his Augustinian Recollect brothers and their communities, never failing to visit them when his many travels took him to places in the United States or overseas where such communities and ministries were to be found.

Cardinal Mahony had pointed out, in his homily preached at the Mass of Christian Burial for the repose of the soul of Bishop Gallegos, that his life had achieved a happy balance between a profound interior union with Jesus Christ and a generous and genuine self-giving. Typical of this kind of spiritual depth and integrity is to be found in a conference that the bishop gave to Hispanic seminarians on the theme of "spirituality." His goal is not so much to define *spirituality* for a particular group of future priests but to share with them, in his own words, "my intimate, personal relation with the Lord as a seminarian, as a priest, and as an Hispanic bishop."[10] The bishop is careful to underscore that, although a spirituality responds to the conditions of a particular culture, its vitality and authenticity rests in the union of these particular forms with the universal church.

He rejects the artificial distinction between the so-called vertical and horizontal approaches to defining spirituality. His concept of "Love one another" surpasses such distinctions, because the love of God necessarily includes love of neighbor and of self. Bishop Alphonse strongly urges the future Hispanic priests to stay close to their cultural roots, to learn from the poor, and to know and to be faithful to the teachings of the church.

The young Catholic Youth Organization leader from Watts who became the Hispanic bishop for the Diocese of Sacramento had a strong sense not only of assisting the undocumented materially and spiritually but, in turn, urging the Hispanic newcomer to contribute to the churches of their new surroundings by giving the gift of their "joyfulness" to their neighbors. The theme of "joy" is very much central to Gallegos's pastoral approach to all the faithful, not only the Hispanics. He mentions that the capacity for joyful celebration, the particular gift that the Mexican brings to his new home, is something to be shared and to be used to bring life to these new surroundings, which are too often burdened by the demands of a consumer society. He is very clear on the topic, as he indicates in a brief written message entitled, "Para Estar Cerca del Reino de los Cielos."[11] He invites his listeners to consider the reasons for joy among Christians and the joyful traditions of celebration that raise the human heart to heaven and bring the family and community together in hope and expectation. Life is hard for the immigrant, but that should be no reason for sadness. There is the joy of life itself, the joy of family, and the healing powers of faith in a loving Father always awaiting our return.

"Love One Another," the Church as One

The homily preached by Bishop Alphonse Gallegos at the annual Chrism Mass (1983), in the presence of Bishop Quinn, the clergy of the diocese, religious, and laity, is a good indicator of his Augustinian-inspired ecclesiology. He shares with his congregation a vision of the church centered in the Eucharist and the oneness of all "who belong to Christ."[12] He reminds the faithful of the leadership of the ordinary and the need for all, priests, religious, and Christian parents, to respond to their vocations with a self-sacrificing generosity as exemplified in the Mass as sacrifice. He emphasizes, as on other occasions, the idea of a vocation not as a "once upon a time occurrence" but rather as an ongoing dialogue with God grounded in prayer and in openness to graced living. Christian vocations are calls to serve and "every form of apostolic life, of either the individual or community, must be in accord with the Gospel."[13] Such service, he explicitly concludes, must be directed to "the Lazarus of the twentieth century who stands at our door."[14] The poor and needy, the migrant and the marginal, represent, in his thinking, occasions calling for united effort, fidelity to the gospel, and prophetic response to the "signs of today."[15]

One of the most moving and explicit declarations of Bishop Alphonse's affirmation of church unity is to be found in his report of his participation in the Eucharistic Congress held in war-torn Nicaragua in November 1986.[16] He had been encouraged by the apostolic delegate in the United States, Archbishop Pio Laghi, to attend the Congress. Prior to arriving at Managua, he paid a visit to the tomb of Archbishop Oscar Romero in El Salvador. In the English language version of the Spanish original, he describes a visit to the tomb of the Archbishop:

> I visited the tomb of our brother, Bishop Oscar Romero, in San Salvador. I simply prayed and meditated in the silent and sacred cathedral that, under the gaze and protection of Most Holy Mary of Guadalupe, this hero of love and liberty be granted eternal rest. Here rests a great and peaceful leader who did not hesitate to risk his life for the most noble and sacred human rights. I offered the Virgin heartfelt thanks for the example of this saint and

immediately recalled the saying of Christ our Teacher: "the Church will be persecuted but will never be defeated."[17]

During the course of his visit he was deeply moved by the response of the faithful to the theme of the Congress, "The Eucharist Fountain of Unity and Reconciliation." Wherever he went during this visit of two weeks, whether in urban or rural churches, he heard the people greet him with the motto of the Congress, "La Iglesia Es Una: La Iglesia Es Una" (The Church Is One, the Church Is One). The bravery of the ordinary Catholic Nicaraguan in the face of a Marxist-oriented attempt to create, with the backing of the state, an "Iglesia popular" encouraged Gallegos to deliver a message of international Catholic solidarity in the common search for peace and unity. In representation of the church in the United States, he spoke of a desire for peace and reconciliation based upon an allegiance "in faith and obedience to our Holy Father."[18] The church as "one" has no frontiers.

Bishop Alphonse carefully avoided politicizing his visit. He would openly give witness when required, such as visiting the prelature of Juigala, seat of the exiled Bishop Pablo Antonio Vega. "There," he writes, "I assured the people of the support and prayers of the Church in the United States, again expressing that we are one Church and one Faith."[19] The style that Alphonse adopted in dealing with provocative political issues was neither confrontational nor compromising; he simply spoke clearly about the teachings of the church. "I could not help but feel the presence of a living Church, manifesting its dynamic faith, a Church alive, a Church that is suffering in a land that is suffering."[20] What most pained this "bishop of the youth" was the absence of young men from the cities and villages that he visited. They had been recruited or forced into one or the other of the two bands in conflict, sometimes pitting brother against brother. He felt deeply the chaos in Nicaragua but was reassured by the thousands of little children whose manifestations of faith accompanied him on this journey of witness to the oneness of the church universal in spite of all the forces of division.

No one perceived more clearly the fidelity of Bishop Gallegos to the church and its doctrines than the ordinary of the Sacramento Diocese, Bishop Francis Quinn. In a communication sent to the apostolic delegate, Archbishop Pio Laghi, he wrote with reference to his auxiliary, "I know of no bishop more loyal to the teaching magisterium of the Church."[21] In the same letter, Bishop Quinn continues, "In the years I have known Bishop Gallegos, I have come to value highly his perception of what the universal Church and what the diocese is."[22] Moreover, "among my consultors, I value his judgment on diocesan decisions above all others."[23] Especially praiseworthy in the auxiliary bishop, according to Bishop Quinn, is his pastoral sense and ability to inspire others to serve the church.

A Gift of Love

Various memorials have been erected to recall the passage of an unusually good man and loving pastor of souls. One of these was a poem written as a "gift of love" within days of the death of Bishop Gallegos by Phil Goldvarg, a social worker in Sacramento. It provides a fitting conclusion to this brief attempt to write a biography of the son of José and Caciana Gallegos.

A GIFT OF LOVE
PARA BISHOP GALLEGOS
Child of God
Child of Earth la Madre
He walked the dirt floor
With migrant worker
The young
Elderly

Lessons in Spirituality

The ill
Hopeless
With low riders
And those
Who have won their struggle
He placed himself in service
To God
To his hermanos y hermanas
Taking to his back
Burden
Upon burden
The multi-oppressions of this world
Confronting injustice with Vision
Beyond ordinary sight
He was the face of Mestizo
Aztec
Toltec
Farm worker
The fearless crossers of El Rio
The Striker
The Protester
He was the face of La familia
He would fall to his knees
To Pray
To plant life in the earth
To lift another from the mud
He had no fear
Except for his brothers and sisters
The assaults on their freedom
His struggle was constant
Never ending
His blood
A river
That nourished the hopeless

Bishop of the Barrio

His fingers
Clawing the rock hard wall of prejudice
His voice
Un grito en la noche
Reaching into the dark cave of broken
Dreams
There is no death for his Spirit
His grito
They will live
They will vibrate in the fields
The streets
In the fearful parts of our hearts
The gift of Bishop Gallegos
Is the circle of giving
Of life

End to end
The hoop of our lives[24]

—Phil Goldvarg

Afterword

Text of the homily by Cardinal Roger Mahony, archbishop of Los Angeles, at Mass of Christian Burial celebrated for Most Rev. Alphonse Gallegos, OAR, DD, auxiliary bishop of Sacramento, Friday, October 11, 1991, 11 a.m., Cathedral of the Blessed Sacrament, Sacramento, California.

A gentle man, loving priest, a caring bishop! Bishop Gallegos entered eternal life in the same fashion that he lived out his life as a priest and as a bishop: helping others, being of service to those with whom he shared his life.

No one would have faulted a 60-year-old bishop for wanting to get out on busy Highway 99 at night and help push a disabled automobile to a safe location. In this case, the bishop was Alphonse Gallegos, and nothing would have been more natural for him than to do exactly what he did last Sunday night.

But this time, his act of generosity cost him his earthly life, and thrust him into that eternal life towards which each one of us longs and yearns. St. Paul's words in this morning's second Scripture came true for Bishop Gallegos: "...all of us are to be changed—in an instant, in the twinkling of an eye, at the sound of the last trumpet." In a real sense, his "twinkling of an eye" took place on an historic, well-traveled central California highway.

Born Feb. 20, 1931, in Albuquerque, New Mexico, Alphonse Gallegos is a fourth-generation American. His parents, Joseph and Caciana Gallegos, brought Alphonse to live some 18 years of his life on Watts Avenue in the heart of the Watts section of South Central Los Angeles. The Gallegos' home housed the five sons and six daughters of Mr. and Mrs. Gallegos—located just four blocks from San Miguel Church where someday Alphonse would serve as pastor.

But his path to priestly life and ministry was not an easy one. Suffering from serious eye deficiency, Alphonse, his family, and his friends prayed through the intercession of St. Lucy, patroness of vision, for help with this seeming obstacle to priestly ordination.

An eye specialist took a special interest in Alphonse and his condition, and in 1948 and 1949 two successful eye surgeries gained him adequate vision to be accepted for priestly studies a year later. It was almost as if Isaiah's prophecy proclaimed in our first Scripture today was meant for Alphonse: "On this mountain the Lord of hosts will destroy the veil that veils all peoples...." Could this possibly be a reference to the veil that poor eyesight brings in its trail?

In 1950 Alphonse entered the Augustinian Recollect Monastery in Kansas City for his novitiate, where he made his simple profession, his solemn profession and his philosophical studies. Completing his theology studies at Tagaste Seminary in New York, he was ordained a priest on May 24, 1958. With immense joy and pride Father Alphonse Gallegos celebrated his first High Mass at San Miguel Parish on June 8, 1958.

The young Father Gallegos served in various pastoral assignments as well as undertaking advanced studies in theology, psychology and religious studies.

In August 1972 Father Gallegos assumed his first pastorate at San Miguel Church in Watts, just a few blocks from where he grew up and where he celebrated his First Mass.

His life and ministry at San Miguel Parish reflected an incredible commitment to Christ, to a deep spirituality, and to a hope-filled proclamation of the Gospel. If joy is the infallible sign of God's presence, then Father Gallegos' life reflected that sign with a dynamism and energy that could not be contained.

About three years after his appointment as pastor, Father Gallegos reflected on the need for joy as an instrument of God's grace: "Watts is an impoverished area, but not a sad area. There is a lot of spirit, a lot of hope. It is a very happy community in spite of everything."

It was evident early on that the vision portrayed by Jesus in today's Gospel was truly that of Father Gallegos: "For I was hungry and you gave me food, I was thirsty and you gave me drink. I was a stranger and you welcomed me, naked and you clothed me. I was ill and you comforted me, in prison and you came to visit me."

The enthusiasm and the challenge of Jesus' words moved Father Alphonse to adopt two important principles that guided his life as pastor and as bishop; first, that one needs a strong spiritual life in order to know Jesus deeply and personally: otherwise, how are we to recognize him in others. And second, that frequent pastoral visits are essential to bringing food and drink to those in need, to discover the stranger and the ill, and to bring comfort to the imprisoned and abandoned.

These two overriding personal principles would be the foundation stones of his life through last Sunday night. It would be hard to imagine any pastor or bishop who more zealously sought to be with his people to bring the joy and the promises of Jesus Christ to them, and to spend himself and be spent for them.

During his term as pastor at San Miguel, Father Gallegos also participated actively with Cardinal Timothy Manning to establish a program for Spanish-speaking permanent deacons—one of the first such programs in the country.

In 1978, Father Gallegos completed his six-year term at San Miguel Parish, and became pastor of Cristo Rey Parish near

Griffith Park area, where he continued with characteristic enthusiasm his outreach to all his parishioners. Continuing to set forth that wonderful vision of Isaiah, Father Gallegos pointed his people to their saving Lord: "Behold our God, to whom we looked to save us! This is the Lord for whom we looked; let us rejoice and be glad that he has saved us!"

In 1979 Father Gallegos was appointed as director of the office of Hispanic Affairs for the California Catholic Conference. And true to form, he continued with his commitment to personal presence: "I will be traveling in the next few months to the various dioceses meeting people and making myself aware."

I first came to know him in his position with the California Catholic Conference, and I was delighted with his joyful enthusiasm for the church's outreach to the growing Hispanic communities across the state. Father Gallegos set in place networks and programs for Hispanic ministry that would become models for the entire nation, networks that continue to this very day.

He was the spark that set in motion the mobile pastoral teams for farmworkers throughout California, as well as the Spanish language radio programs that reached migrant farmworkers in California and in Mexico.

It was not unusual to find Father Gallegos out on Franklin Boulevard on Friday and Saturday nights talking to the low-riders, blessing their cars, encouraging the young drivers; and meeting with them at St. Rose's Rectory to help them through a variety of problems and concerns.

Appointed as Auxiliary Bishop for the Diocese of Sacramento in the fall of 1981, Bishop Alphonse Gallegos was ordained a bishop by Bishop Francis Quinn on November 4—the feast of St. Charles Borromeo, that wonderfully pastoral bishop of Milan in Italy.

His episcopal motto, "Love One Another," reflected the call of Jesus in the Gospels and the Rule of St. Augustine, a motto placed on the belt of the habit of the Order of Augustinian Recollects. His coat of arms was itself a collage of all that Bishop Gallegos held dear in his life as a fervent disciple of Jesus Christ and as a sharer in his priesthood.

Bishop Gallegos was then to live out almost 10 full years as a bishop in the service of the Lord and the church whom he loved so deeply. This decade of loving service to the people of Sacramento, in close collaboration with Bishop Quinn, was a continuation of that vision and dynamism which Jesus described for us in our Gospel.

Ever on the move, always anxious to be with his people, devotedly serving as shepherd to all, especially the poor and powerless, Bishop Alphonse Gallegos lived to the fullest all that Jesus proclaimed in Matthew's Gospel today.

Very possibly in the very action of his death Bishop Gallegos added just one more virtuous action to Jesus' own listing in the Gospel: "My car had stalled on the highway, and you got out to help push me."

A gentle man, a loving priest, a caring bishop has now heard those very words of Jesus: "Come! You have my Father's blessing! Inherit the kingdom prepared for you!"

Notes

Chapter 1   Early Years

1. "Surgical Correction of Extreme Myopia. Report of a Case," Doctors' Hospital Bulletin, Vol. 7, Book 10, December 1949, Doctors' Hospital, 325 W. Jefferson Blvd., Los Angeles, CA.

2. C. Fernández-Shaw, *The Hispanic Presence in North America from 1492 to Today,* trans. Alfonso Bertodano Stourton et al. (New York: Facts on File, 1991), p. 201. "New Mexico retains its Hispanic atmosphere, while at the same time, contributing its own flavor to the great melting-pot of American culture."

Chapter 2   Seeing with the Heart

1. Letter from Bishop Gallegos to Fr. Placido Lanz, OAR, October 8, 1982. Provincial archives, West Orange, NJ.

2. Fr. A. Gallegos, "Why I Became a Recollect Augustinian," n.d. Provincial archives, West Orange, NJ.

3. Letter from Rev. Jim Elmer, OAR, to the prior of St. Augustine Missionary Seminary, Kansas City, KS. No date is given, but from the contents, the letter appears to be contemporary to the surgery of 1948. Provincial archives.

4. Rev. Alphonse Gallegos, Master of Novices, "Novitiate Training in a Time of Change," Provincial archives. No date is given, but, since it is signed "Master of Novices," it might be assumed that it dates from the period 1967-1969.

5. Gallegos, "Why I Became a Recollect Augustinian."

6. Chapter report from the Monastery of St. Augustine to the major superior following solemn profession in September 1954. Provincial archives.

7. Letter of Dr. H. G. Blasdel to Alphonse Gallegos, September 21, 1955. Provincial archives.

8. House chapter book, Tagaste Monastery, Suffern, NY, January 18, 1958, p. 25.

9. Ibid., p. 32

10. Libro de cosas notables, 1929-1967, San Miguel Parish, June 10, 1960, p. 122. Provincial archives.

Chapter 3   Preaching the Word

1. Letter from Ramón Castroviejo, MD, to Bro. Alfonso Gallegos, February 25, 1960. Provincial archives.

2. Letter from Caciana Gallegos to "my dear son," May 2, 1960. Held by Mrs. Senaida Kane, Albuquerque, NM.

3. The invitation card to this event refers to the "Saint Joseph Wake," a playful and literal translation of the *Velorio* in honor of San José.

Chapter 4   Watts Is "Out of Control"

1. Libro de cosas notables, 1929-1967, San Miguel Parish, August 10, 1965, p. 13. Provincial archives.

2. Libro de cosas notables, 1971, San Miguel Parish, pp. 8-9. Provincial archives.

3. Letter to Very Rev. James D. McGuire, prior provincial, July 10, 1972. Provincial archives.

4. Center for Applied Research to the Apostolate, Apostolate to the Spanish-Speaking, "San Miguel Parish, Los Angeles," Vol. I, September 1974, 120-25.

5. Letter from Bro. Michael Stechmann, OAR, to Richard Alcala, April 12, 1995. Provincial archives.

6. Letter from a parishioner of San Miguel to the prior provincial, May 25, 1978. Provincial archives.

7. San Miguel Elementary School Self-Evaluation, April 14-15, 1975, p. 29.

8. Letter from Rev. Alphonse Gallegos to Rev. Msgr. Benjamin G. Hawkes, August 15, 1977. Provincial archives.

9. *Low-riders* is the term applied to the owners of automobiles especially designed and reconstructed to emphasize a close-to-the-ground chassis and a highly decorated car body, a popular hobby among the young Latinos of the Southwest.

10. Moisés Sandoval, "Bishop for Youth," *Revista Maryknoll* (1982), 13.

11. Formation chapter report, Monastery of St. Augustine, 1954. Kansas City, KS.

12. Ibid.

13. "Greetings to Father Provincial," San Miguel Parish Council, apparently written in 1978, the year of Fr. Gallegos's transfer to Cristo Rey Parish. Provincial archives.

14. Letter from Timothy Cardinal Manning to Most Rev. James D. McGuire, OAR, May 9, 1978. Provincial archives.

15. Homily of Roger Cardinal Mahony, *The Catholic Herald*, October 16, 1991, p. 10.

Chapter 5   A Call to a Wider Ministry

1. Letter from Very Rev. James D. McGuire, OAR, Prior General, to his Eminence Timothy Cardinal Manning, June 9, 1978. Provincial archives.

2. Letter from Bishop John Ward to Rev. Francis E. Peluso, OAR, prior provincial, Augustinian Recollects, July 9, 1981. Provincial archives.

3. Journal of Bishop Alphonse Gallegos, October 1, 1979, p. 100. Provincial archives.

4. Ibid., October 4, 1979.

5. Ibid., March 12, 1980, p. 111.

6. Ibid., June 23, 1980, p. 115.

7. R. J. Laine, "The Lord and the Lowrider," *City Lights* (Sacramento), p. 7.

8. Journal, August 4, 1981, p. 127.

9. Ibid., August 23, 1981, p. 128.

10. Ibid., August 26-27, 1981, pp. 129-30.

11. Ibid., September 1, 1981, p. 131.

12. Bishop-Elect Alphonse Gallegos, September 1, 1981. Archives, Diocese of Sacramento.

13. Ibid.

14. Ibid., quoting *Rule of St. Augustine,* chap. 1.

Chapter 6   The Joy of Being Catholic

1. R. Witt, "Hispanic Bishop Picked in Capital," *Sacramento Bee,* September 2, 1981, p. B3.

2. The Gallegos surname surfaces in early colonial times in New Mexico. Cf. Fray Angélico Chávez, *Origins of New Mexico Families: A Genealogy of the Spanish Colonial People* (Santa Fe, NM: Museum of New Mexico Press, 1992).

3. The letter was published in 1988 in a bilingual edition as *The Joy of Being Catholic/El Gozo de Ser Católico,* California Catholic Conference.

4. "The Hispanic Presence Challenge and Commitment" (Washington, DC: USCC, 1983) and "The Bishops Speak with the Virgin. Pastoral Letter of the Hispanic Bishops of the U.S." (Washington, DC: USCC, 1982).

5. Letter to Rev. Francis E. Peluso, OAR, prior provincial, March 8, 1982. Provincial archives.

6. Testimony of Olympia V. Nuñez in response to the "Questionnaire Concerning the Life and Works of Bishop Alphonse Gallegos, OAR (deceased)."

7. Ibid.

8. "Recuerdo del Vigesimo Aniversario 12 Diciembre 1978," Santuario de Nuestra Señora de Guadalupe, Sacramento, CA.

9. A typewritten copy of the "Report of the Problem of the Church and the Spanish-Speaking in the Diocese of Sacramento

(February 1963)" has been made available by Fr. William Breault, SJ, archivist of the Catholic Diocese of Sacramento.

10. "Pastoral Proposal" I, Our Lady of Guadalupe Church, March 11, 1965. Archives, Diocese of Sacramento.

11. Ibid., "Pastoral Proposal" II, 1. d.

12. Letter to Fr. John Gruben, OAR, prior provincial, Province of St. Augustine, from Gerald and Reseanne Lalumiere and children, August 27, 2002. Provincial archives.

13. "Personal reflections of John Madrid regarding the Most Reverend Bishop Alphonse Gallegos," October 17, 2003. Provincial archives.

14. Interview by author with Patricia Villavazgo, La Palma, CA.

15. Stuart Aase, *Sacramento Union,* May 11, 1987, p. A2.

16. Ibid.

17. Ibid.

18. House chronicle, Cristo Rey Parish, October 1990, p. 75. Provincial archives.

19. Moisés Sandoval, "Bishop for Youth," *Revista Maryknoll* (1982), p. 13.

20. Ibid.

21. B. Armbruster, "Bishop Takes to Fields, Streets to Meet His Flock," *Advocate* (The Newspaper of the Roman Catholic Archdiocese of Newark, New Jersey) Vol. 31, no. 35, September 1, 1982, p. 4.

22. Homily of Roger Cardinal Mahony, *The Catholic Herald,* October 16, 1991, p. 10.

23. Statement of Bishop Alphonse Gallegos, auxiliary of Sacramento, July 1986.

24. Hon. Robert T. Matsui, House of Representatives, "A Tribute to the Late Bishop Alphonse Gallegos," *Congressional Record,* Vol. 137, no. 145, Washington, DC, October 8, 1991.

25. Michael Wood, "Bishop Gallegos Dies in Tragic Auto Accident," *Catholic Herald,* October 16, 1991, p. 11.

26. Conference of Bishop Alfonso Gallegos, taped at the 1 Congreso Católico Carismático, Sacramento, CA, September 20-22, 1991.

27. Testimony of Olympia Nuñez.

28. Letter from Maria J. Navarro to Fr. John Gruben, OAR, prior provincial, Province of St. Augustine, August 27, 2002. Provincial archives.

29. "Bishops Protest Train Carrying Weapons," *New York Times,* February 24, 1984, p. 10.

30. *The Catholic Herald,* December 14, 1991, p. 1.

31. Ibid., p. 18.

32. "Report of the Problem of the Church and the Spanish-Speaking."

33. *Diocesan Pastoral Plan for Hispanic Ministry/Plan Pastoral Diocesano para el Ministerio Hispano,* Bilingual Edition, Diocese of Sacramento, April 1991, p. 8.

34. Ibid., p. 10.

35. Ibid., p. 11.

36. Ibid., p. 6.

37. Letter of Bishop Francis Quinn, bishop of Sacramento, to "Dearly Beloved People," published in the *Diocesan Pastoral Plan for Hispanic Ministry/Plan Pastoral Diocesano,* p. 1.

Chapter 7   Gentle Man, Loving Priest, Caring Bishop

1. A complete coverage of the event from Ruiz's perspective was published a year later in Spanish in *El Heraldo Católico,* Diócesis de Sacramento, Domingo 4 de Octubre de 1992, pp. 1, 7.

2. A complete description of the accident was published in the Metro section of the *The Sacramento Bee,* October 7, 1991.

3. Edgar Sanchez, "From All Quarters Friends Bid Goodbye to Gallegos," *The Sacramento Bee,* October 11, 1991, p. B1.

4. Homily at the vigil service for Bishop Alphonse Gallegos, OAR, delivered by Fr. John J. Oldfield, OAR, prior provincial of the Augustinian Recollects, *The Catholic Herald,* October 16, 1991, p. 15.

5. Homily by Roger Cardinal Mahony, *The Catholic Herald,* October 11, 1991, p. 10.

6. Ibid.

7. Bishop Francis A. Quinn, "A Tribute to Bishop Gallegos," *The Catholic Herald,* October 16, 1991, p. 13.

8. David Barton and Ramon Coronado, "Cathedral Packed for Bishop's Memorial Mass," *The Sacramento Bee,* October 12, 1991, p. B1.

Chapter 8   Burnt Tortillas and a Statue

1. Bob Sylva, "'Bishop of the Barrio' Play an Act of Faith and Charity," *The Sacramento Bee,* February 11, 1995, p. A2.

2. Ibid.

3. *The Catholic Herald,* October 16, 1991, p. 12.

4. Sermon of Bishop Gallegos entitled, "Mary, Mother of the Poor," n.d.

5. Unveiling Program for statue of Bishop Alfonso Gallegos, February 23, 1997, Sacramento, CA.

6. An account of the dedication of the Gallegos statue is included in *The Catholic Herald,* March 8, 1997, p. 1.

Chapter 9   Lessons in Spirituality

1. Preface, *Rule of St. Augustine.*

2. Ibid., *Rule* 1. 2.

3. "Religious in the Twentieth Century," n.d. Provincial archives.

4. Ibid., p. III.

5. Personal record of Rev. Alphonse Gallegos. Archives, Diocese of Sacramento.

6. Conversation with Olympia Nuñez, secretary of Bishop Gallegos, January 21, 2003.

7. "Religious in the Twentieth Century," p. IV.

8. Ibid.

9. Ibid.

10. Conference by Bishop Gallegos, "Espiritualidad de los Seminaristas Hispanos." Provincial archives.

11. Sermon by Bishop Gallegos, "Para Estar Cerca del Reino de los Cielos," n.d. Provincial archives.

12. "Chrism Talk to Priests," Holy Thursday, March 24, 1983, p. 1. Provincial archives.

13. Ibid., p. 4.

14. Ibid.

15. Ibid.

16. There are two documents relating this visit to Nicaragua, one in English *(Where Are the Children?)* and one in Spanish *(Una Peregrinación que Nunca Olvidaré)*. Both were written in November 1986. Provincial archives.

17. *Una Peregrinación,* p. 3. The original Spanish text, published in English translation by the author of this book, is as follows: "Visité la tumba de nuestro hermano, el Obispo Oscar Romero, en San Salvador. No hice más que orar y meditar en aquella catedral silenciosa y sagrada que otorga, bajo la mirada y complaciencia de María Santísima de Guadalupe, la eterna paz a este héroe del amor, de libertad. Reposa impresionante, un gran lider pacífico, que no temió arriesgar su vida por los derechos más nobles y sagrados del hombre. Di sentidas gracias a la Virgen por el ejemplo de este santo, y recordé instantáneamente aquella advertencia de Cristo Nuestro Maestro: 'la Iglesia será perseguida, pero jamás será vencida.'"

18. *Where Are the Children?,* p. 2.

19. Ibid., p. 5.

20. Ibid., p. 3.

21. Letter of Francis A. Quinn, bishop of Sacramento, to Most Rev. Pio Laghi, August 30, 1985 (No. PD 169/85/2). Archives, Diocese of Sacramento.

22. Ibid.

23. Ibid.

24. Phil Goldvarg, "A Gift of Love para Bishop Gallegos," *The Catholic Herald,* October 16, 1991, p. 13.